HOW TO WIN THE CONSTITUTIONAL WAR
and give both sides what they want

Tony Abbott, a former Rhodes Scholar, is the Member for Warringah in the
Federal Parliament and a Parliamentary Secretary in the Howard
Government. Before entering Parliament, he was Executive Director of
Australians for Constitutional Monarchy. His first book, *The Minimal
Monarchy*, was a defence of the existing constitutional arrangements. This
book is a proposal for constitutional reform that builds on the strengths
of our existing systems.

T0363749

This book is dedicated to Margaret Olley AO
for her support and encouragement.

HOW TO WIN THE CONSTITUTIONAL WAR
and give both sides
what they want

TONY ABBOTT

Published by Australians for Constitutional Monarchy
in association with Wakefield Press

Australians for Constitutional Monarchy
in associaion with Wakefield Press

First published 1997

Cover illustration by Stephen Bowers, Adelaide.
Book designed and typeset by Tabloid Pty Ltd, Adelaide.
Printed and bound by Hyde Park Press, Adelaide.

ISBN 1 86254 433 6

CONTENTS

ACKNOWLEDGMENTS

Originally, this book was going to be a revised and up-dated version of *The Minimal Monarchy*, re-published to coincide with the People's Constitutional Convention. I am indebted to my editor, Christopher Pearson, for persuading me that the constitutional debate needed to be extended and the argument developed lest the Convention become a slanging match between two sides with pre-conceived ideas. Hence, this book is about modernising the system as well as defending it.

Since the beginning of this debate, supporters of the Constitution have been accused of "stone-walling" any suggestion for change. This is my attempt to take the debate forward: to develop new constitutional arrangements which recognise important elements of the republican critique while preserving our existing system of government.

This new book would not have been possible without the support of my wife, Margaret. I should also thank the Parliamentary Library and the office of the Clerk of the House (in particular Indra Kuruppu and Ian Cochrane) for their invaluable assistance at very short notice. I have tried (perhaps not always successfully) to do justice to the wise counsel of my friend and former boss, Lloyd Waddy.

This book is dedicated to Margaret Olley, a member of the Foundation Council of Australians for Constitutional Monarchy, and through her to all the men and women of ACM who, when others were giving up, maintained their faith in Australian institutions..

CHAPTER ONE

Sleepwalking towards a republic

IN mid-1997, I met a university political science student who had just been elected 'youth governor' of her State by a 'parliament' of young Australians. It was six years after the formation of the Australian Republican Movement dedicated to making Australia a republic by 2001, five years after the then-Prime Minister had declared his support for a republic by the turn of the century and some months after the new Prime Minister had announced a people's convention to consider Australia's constitutional future.

'Should Australia become a republic?' I asked. 'Oh yes,' she said with great enthusiasm '... because we shouldn't be tied to another country'. She said her friends had thought about it 'a lot'. To the further question 'do you want a politician as president?', she looked blank and then said that she wasn't sure.

On constitutional matters, her attitude reflects a common mixture of confidence and ignorance. Becoming a republic and substituting an elected president for an appointed governor-general is by far the biggest constitutional change Australians have ever been asked to make. Leading republicans' attempts to re-write the Constitution to replace the Governor-General with a president have involved adding, deleting or amending more than 70 clauses in the existing 128 clause document. On any argument, this is the nearest thing to a constitutional 'big bang' Australia has ever contemplated – yet 'within coo-ee' of a national vote, even relatively well-informed Australians have only the haziest idea of what it's all about.

Into this atmosphere of strong feeling mixed with ignorance, came the death of Princess Diana on August 31. Everyone would always remember, said Kim Beazley, where they were when they heard the news. If, as the critics often claimed, the monarchy had become a soap opera, Diana's death showed just how powerful the drama could be. For a fortnight, millions of Australians could talk of little else but the rights and wrongs of one woman and one family. Dozens of places became unofficial shrines with photographs of the late princess and wreaths with 'we'll never forget you' messages.

Whether it was Diana's concern for people living with AIDS and lepers, the Royals' inability to open their hearts to a young wife they couldn't understand, or Earl Spencer's scornful panegyric which most stirred people, the remarkable public passions of that first fortnight in September 1997 helped to emphasise our ill-preparedness to consider the future of the Australian Constitution. Constitutional change should not hinge on our reactions to a funeral – any more than it should be affected by the Olympic Games or the Year 2000.

Even if, as many republicans argue, turning the Governor-General into some kind of elected president is only a symbolic change (like two people who live together deciding to get married), it should not lightly be undertaken. As Margaret Thatcher once said:

Those who imagine that a politician would make a better figurehead than a hereditary monarch should make the acquaintance of more politicians.

Sydney Morning Herald, **21 November, 1995**

'Remove the foreign Queen' say republicans. 'Protect the Constitution' say monarchists. Yet how can voters make intelligent decisions about Australia's constitutional future when 50% (according to a 1988 study undertaken for the Constitutional Commission) are not even sure that Australia has a constitution and 82% (according to the Federal Government's Civics Education Group report in 1994) know nothing about the Constitution's content? Perhaps this is not surprising – as just 19% of Year 12 students in NSW (and just 6% in Victoria) now study history.

At the moment, Australians are sleep-walking towards constitutional change. We need to wake up fast and re-learn the strengths of our existing Constitution: to make any change with our eyes open; or (as I argue in this book) to address widespread unease about our existing constitutional arrangements without compromising our system of government.

Not since the Federation debates of the 1890s have Australians had to make such a big decision about our system of government. In those days there may have been less controversy about the merits of change but, perhaps, just as much credulity and ignorance about the details. Mungo MacCallum quotes a pro-Federation speaker who is supposed to have told a Tasmanian audience that:

> If you vote for the (Federation) Bill you will found a great and glorious nation under the bright Southern Cross and meat will be cheaper and you will live to see the Australian race dominate the Southern seas and you will have a market for both potatoes and apples and your sons shall reap the grand heritage of nationhood...

The most important debate in Australia today

It was fatuous then – and it is nonsense now – to say that constitutional change, of itself, will make Australians happy, healthy and prosperous. At one level, constitutional debate is irrelevant to Australia's practical problems. The point has often been made that becoming a republic will not take a dollar off the national debt, remove one person from the unemployment queue, nor make black and white Australians feel better about each other. Even so, it is by far the most important debate taking place in Australia today because – as the residents of Hong Kong are only too well aware – systems of government eventually make a big difference to the way people live.

When historians come to consider Australia at this time, the constitutional debate is likely to loom larger than the big economic questions because it touches the essence of what it means to be an Australian. It will be more important than the question of who owned the *Sydney Morning Herald*. Yet very few people are talking about it across the back fence or on the way to work.

Australians for Constitutional Monarchy has 18,000 signed-up supporters. The Australian Republican Movement says it has 6000 members. Such figures are dwarfed even by the membership of political parties – yet these are the organisations which will contest the constitutional votes which will decide Australia's constitutional future.

Compared to the constitutional debate, tax reform is relatively easy. Tax reform involves detailed analysis and hard choices. But it is not an argument involving the fundamentals of our system of government nor the constitutional symbols which help to shape the self-perceptions of the nation. Even so, attitudes to tax reform still tend to boil down to deeply held instincts about taxation as a means to help the needy or to burden the successful.

Whether to keep a crown which is an important part of the Australian tradition or to dump a monarch who is said to shackle us to the past is an altogether more challenging issue. Is the French republic a more 'successful' nation than the Dutch monarchy? How is success to be determined, whatdifference has a crown made and how much does any difference matter? Such questions are hard enough for detached observers to grapple with – and outsiders have less emotional stake in the answers. This is the Pandora's Box which Paul Keating opened when he claimed, in effect, that Australia's constitutional emperor had no clothes.

In a sense, whether people are monarchists or republicans is akin to whether Christians are Roman Catholic or Anglican. It is a question of faith. It turns on upbringing, experience, emotional disposition, personal quirks. It is intensely personal and difficult-to-argue-about. It often defies analysis according to the usual political and cultural indicators. Still, even believers who do not need reasons and sceptics who cannot accept reasons may benefit from an attempt to muster an argument. Aquinas' 'proofs' of the existence of God were a valuable contribution even to an argument which can never be settled.

For years, Australians could be monarchists or republicans in private. Life went on regardless of one's attitude to the Constitution. Like it or not, the monarchy was part of our public furniture. But the genie is out of the bottle and the constitutional state of nature must now be re-considered. We have to make a public as well as a private choice. So we need to find means of public discourse which weigh the merits of both positions – without insulting the faith of either side.

'Constitutionalists' not 'monarchists'

Even the terminology can be misleading. Most 'republicans' say they have no problem with the Queen herself nor with the Australian system of government. They just want to address the problem of the 'foreign head of state'. These days, 'monarchists' are more concerned with the Constitution than the Crown. Generally speaking, their attitude reflects pride in the Australian constitutional order as much as devotion to the monarch herself. Perhaps defenders of the existing Australian Constitution are stuck with the 'monarchist' tag like a schoolyard nickname – but 'constitutionalist' (in the sense of reluctance to tamper with the core document of the nation) would be a more accurate term.

There is a sense in which republicans are playing for constitutional 'keeps'. One can support the monarchy today without any obligation to support it once, for instance, Prince Charles becomes king. Republicans, however, lack the luxury of being able to change their minds. A referendum vote to keep the constitutional status quo is not irreversible. A vote to become a republic would be final – if only because re-creating a structure which has taken 1,000 years to evolve would be like trying to re-build a coral reef. In this sense, even ardent republicans should be careful about going too far, too fast.

The finality of change – should it be embraced – means that Australians need to explore more thoroughly the strengths of the system we have as well as its alternatives. The constitutional debate is now more important than it was two years ago (when I produced *The Minimal Monarchy*) because it is finally moving from media speculation into a decision-making process. The time to decide is coming, ready-or-not.

Changed circumstances demand a changed book. Notwithstanding *The Minimal Monarchy's* back-cover claim to make its point 'without resorting to rhetoric', there was an insistent anti-Keating tone that would now be out-of-place. To a considerable extent, this book mines from the old book but the material is re-worked and re-organised rather than simply repeated. The old book was a defence of the existing system. The new one is an attempted solution to the constitutional conundrum which respects the strengths of our existing system while coming to grips with the emotional power of the desire for change.

In *The Minimal Monarchy*, I said:

> If we are to keep the Crown, we must relearn the reasons why. And if we are to reject the cornerstone of our constitutional system, we must at least know what we are doing. It's increasingly clear, that if change is to occur, Paul Keating will not be its only father. Successful nations need better arguments for change and cohesive republics need more credible authors.

Half-way through the Howard Government's first term, the debate Keating began is finally coming to a head. As a nation, we cannot dither endlessly at the banks of this constitutional Rubicon. At the Constitutional Convention, the Government will need a position of its own – either to open debate or to resolve a deadlock. Coming to the Convention with, so to speak, its mind open but its mouth closed is not really an option (even for a government determined to avoid forcing the issue). 'You tell us what do to' (should that be the Government's position) would be altogether too reminiscent of a former British prime minister's lament 'of course I must follow them, I am their leader'.

The saying: 'if it ain't broke don't fix it', has the corollary: 'if it is broke, fix it – don't throw it away'. There is nothing wrong with our existing Constitution except the fact that more than half the Australian people (not very passionately and not necessarily now) want change. It's not, by and large, that they are against the Queen nor for a republic; they just want Australia to stand up for itself and have been told that becoming a republic might be a way of showcasing our county's strengths. As Abraham Lincoln once reminded his compatriots 'a house divided against itself cannot stand'. This book invites republicans to consider the merits of what we have. It also offers a compromise which enables both sides to claim a sort-of-victory and which, I hope, may restore the Australian Constitution to a place of uncontentious honour.

The compromise tries to address the republican critique without adopting the republic solution. It is an attempt at an Australian solution to an Australian problem which builds on what we have rather than on models which may (or may not) have worked well in other countries. Essentially, I have tried to express the reality of Australia's current constitutional position which (a little like the Australian people) is an amalgam of several constitutional traditions which we have made uniquely our own.

CHAPTER TWO

The role of the Crown in the Australian Constitution

T HE Australian Constitution is based on the Crown – not because our constitutional founders were in awe of Queen Victoria but because the concept of the Crown is the foundation stone of the Westminster system. This is not to say that the Australian system of government hinges on the Queen. Rather, the concept of the Crown helps to shape the other elements in our constitutional life.

At the time of Federation, British constitutional history essentially concerned the evolution of the person of the monarch into the legal concept of the Crown. Some time during the 17th and 18th centuries, the 'Crown' ceased to be shorthand for the king and became a metaphor for a system of government under the law.

The 'Crown' as it was known to Deakin, Parkes, Griffith, Barton and the others who drafted the Australian Constitution had almost nothing to do with the human personality of the Queen because the charismatic personal Crown of the Middle Ages had long given way to the 'dignified' Crown recognised by Bagehot as the embodiment of people and state.

Hence the term 'Queen' as used in the Constitution meant

more than 'Queen Victoria'. Queen Victoria was merely the occupier of the office for the time being. The powers given to 'the Queen', for instance, did not die with the Queen Empress (a few months after Federation) but referred to a constitutional office rather than the individual who happened to occupy the throne.

When he went line-by-line through the existing Australian Constitution – making only such additions, amendments and deletions as necessary to produce a 'minimalist' republic – Malcolm Turnbull was forced to make more than 70 changes to a 128 clause document. The pervasive presence of the Crown in the Australian Constitution does not mean, of course, that the Queen runs the Australian Government. It means, rather, that the idea of the Crown as the State, the Queen as the embodiment of the people and, most importantly, the Governor-General as the representative of the executive arm of government are the constitutional foundation stones of the Australian polity.

It was the intention of our constitutional founders to produce a Westminster democracy where the people's representatives worked through the Crown to establish the peace, order and good government of the Commonwealth of Australia. But even in 1901 there was no sense in which the Queen (or her representative) was supposed to exercise the actual government of the country. Even in England, the Queen reigned but did not rule. Here, she could hardly be said to reign at all because the Australian Constitution expressly declared that all her (mostly nominal) powers were to be exercised by the Governor-General of Australia.

Republicans frequently draw attention to section 59 of the Australian Constitution, which gives the Queen 12 months to disallow a law duly passed by the Australian Parliament. What looks like a right of royal veto was actually inserted to give the British Government (acting in the Queen's name) the ability to over-ride the Australian Parliament. It was a dead letter even in 1901, has never been used, and could easily be removed in an act of constitutional spring-cleaning. Nowadays, it could only be used on the advice of the Queen's Australian ministers – which is why no-one has ever bothered to remove it. And this is the only section of the Constitution to give the Queen notional power other than that which the Governor-General exercises in her name.

Unlike the United States' Constitution, whose draftsmen had just fought a long war to secure their right to establish a constitution of their own, the Australian Constitution was the product of a hundred years of peaceful evolution. It was drafted by Australians, for Australians, in Australia and was enshrined as an Act of the British Parliament simply because that was the legal requirement of establishing a new nation. It is highly significant that the Constitution provided for its own amendment – not through further British Acts of Parliament (like the Canadian Constitution drafted a three decades earlier) – but only through a referendum of the Australian people.

The birth certificate of a nation

The Constitution did not derive its popular legitimacy from the passage of a British Act – but from the support of the Australian people voting in plebiscites in every State. Although Australia's constitutional draftsmen were ready to accommodate some amendments at the request of the Imperial Government (such as permitting appeals to the Privy Council), they had no doubt that they were writing the 'birth certificate of a nation' as Sir Isaac Isaacs put it (rather than creating a 'rule book for a colony', as Turnbull has described the Australian Constitution). The Commonwealth of Australia Constitution Act was only passed at all because the people of the Australian States-to-be requested the British Parliament to do so.

11

The Constitution is a distinctively Australian document. For one thing, the new nation christened itself the 'Commonwealth' of Australia (despite the term's Cromwellian and republican overtones) rather than 'dominion' as the Canadians had done 30 years earlier. At the time of Federation, the foreign policy of the British Empire was supposed to be conducted exclusively through London. Canada actually lacked the constitutional power, under the Constitution established by the British North America Act of 1863, to pursue its own foreign policy. Australia's constitutional founders were well aware of this and the fact that they inserted a specific constitutional power over 'external affairs' demonstrates that their focus was Australian as well as Imperial. The new Australian Government subsequently showed its independent spirit – much to the annoyance of Whitehall – by inviting the United States Fleet to visit Sydney without going through the British Foreign Office.

Section 61 of the Constitution vested the executive powers of the Crown in the Governor-General. In fact, the Australian Governor-General is a rather more significant constitutional figure than the British monarch. Bagehot has famously described the Crown's prerogatives as the right to 'be consulted, to encourage and to warn'. The Queen has great moral authority and British prime ministers have often testified to the insights into the workings of government gained from weekly visits to Buckingham Palace. Under the unwritten UK Constitution, however, the Queen can do no more than select as prime minister someone with the ability to command a majority on the floor of Parliament. Since the Tory Party adopted formal ballots for the leadership, the question of 'who might be acceptable to the Palace' is no longer asked – so a hung Parliament in which no-one could cobble together a coalition is the most credible scenario in which the

Queen might have real discretion over whom to choose as her prime minister. Her choice, of course, would only last as long as Parliament supported it.

By contrast, the words of the Australian Constitution give the Governor-General explicit power: to command the armed forces, to summon and prorogue Parliament; to appoint ministers to serve at his or her pleasure; and to sign bills passed by the Parliament into law. By the conventions governing the Crown, these powers are exercised on the advice of the Prime Minister (who commands a majority in parliament) – except when the Prime Minister is acting or threatening to act in breach of the Constitution. In these rare circumstances, the Governor-General is obliged to act as guardian of the Constitution.

In Britain, the Constitution is essentially what the Parliament says it is – which means that a prime minister with a majority in the House of Commons can virtually do what he likes. One of Australia's strengths is a constitution which is much less at the mercy of the Prime Minister of the day. It's a legendarily-hard-to-change legal document which frequently stands in the way of prime ministers-in-a-hurry. Normally, the High Court is called upon to judge the constitutionality of government actions. Still, as the nominal chief executive of such a Commonwealth, the Australian Governor-General is rather more likely than the Queen herself to be called upon to act as constitutional umpire.

This is because the UK House of Lords can only delay legislation. By contrast, the Australian Senate has (in all but one respect) co-equal powers with the House of Representatives and a deadlock between the two Houses could require the Governor-General's intervention. The events centred on 11 November, 1975 were a demonstration – not of the Queen's power over the Australian body politic – but of the Governor-

General's role, under the Australian Constitution, in resolving political crises.

A constitutional umpire

In any event, by 1975 the Crown was a different juridical conception to the 'Crown' under which the colonies had united in 1901. At the time of Federation, constitutional theory enshrined the concept of the 'indivisible Crown'. Today, even republican-minded constitutional authorities acknowledge the existence of the separate 'crowns' of the UK, Canada, Australia, New Zealand and so on. In 1901, Australians were under the British Crown and the Governor-General was an Englishman representing the interests of the Imperial Government. Today, the Queen of Australia is represented by a distinguished Australian citizen representing the people in the name of the Crown.

The Statute of Westminster, negotiated between the representatives of Canada, South Africa, Australia, New Zealand and the United Kingdom and passed by the British Parliament in 1931, was a declaration that – henceforth – the Crown would have the same relationship to the Dominion Governments as it had to the Government of the UK. The role of the Crown in Australia would be the same as the role of the Crown in Britain and the monarch's representative at Yarralumla would exercise the same royal prerogatives 'to be consulted, to encourage and to warn' with respect to the Lodge as the occupant of Buckingham Palace exercised with respect to Number 10 Downing Street.

In other words, the Australian Crown was no less sovereign in Australia than the British Crown was sovereign in the United Kingdom. The appointment of a UK High Commissioner, who thenceforth represented the British Government in Canberra, reflected the Governor-General's new role as representative of the Australian Crown rather than representative of the British Crown (and, in effect, agent of the British Government). The fact that it took Australia a full decade to pass complementary legislation shows how lightly we wore our imperial 'yoke'. Yet even if we failed to recognise it legally until 1942 (and generally continued to ignore constitutional reality thereafter) Australia was completely independent from the moment Britain acknowledged our own local sovereignty.

The Statute of Westminster was the defining moment in Australia's relationship with the Crown. It marked the end of the British Crown in Australia and the beginning of the Australian Crown. Henceforth, it was the Australian monarch (rather than the UK Queen) sitting at the apex of our Constitution – who happened, of course, also to be monarch of Britain, Canada, New Zealand and various other places. The person was the same but the rules, powers, advisers, and spheres of action were totally separate for each country.

The Queen did not become Queen of Australia when the Menzies Government specifically added 'Australia' to her list of realms under the Royal Style and Titles Act of 1954 nor when the Whitlam Government declared her to be 'Queen of Australia', no more and no less, in 1973. She became Queen of Australia the moment she acceded to the throne by virtue of the Australian Constitution. Her Grandfather had been King of Great Britain and, as such, was the sovereign of many nations. She was the Queen of many different nations – of which Britain was simply one. Consultations with the Australian Government (as well as the other Dominion Governments) preceded the abdication of Edward VIII in recognition of this changed constitutional understanding of the relationship of the Crown to its various realms.

The Queen of Australia

The Statute of Westminster illustrates the way our Constitution can evolve even while its words remain the same. The Constitution's preamble states the desire of the then colonies to become 'one indivisible Federal Commonwealth under the Crown of Great Britain and Ireland'. Even though our Constitution has not changed, the Crown has. What was once the Crown of Great Britain, Ireland and possessions and dependencies beyond the sea has separated into its constituent parts, and the Crown pertaining to Australia is now the Australian Crown. As a totally independent nation, Australians alone control the nature of the Australian Crown. No-one else has that power (even though, hitherto, we have always chosen to accept the monarch of the United Kingdom with the UK's disqualifications).

Malcolm Turnbull has suggested that if Britain became a republic, the British president would become monarch of Australia by virtue of the operation of the Australian Constitution. This literalist reading of the Constitution is plainly incorrect. Such a dogmatic interpretation might have left Australia monarch-less in 1948 when the monarch ceased to reign over (all) Ireland and therefore ceased to be precisely as described in our Constitution. In the event that Britain became a republic, the Australian monarch would continue on the throne (regardless of developments in a juridically separate realm) until Australians decided otherwise.

The most recent case of royal interference in Australian affairs – King George V's short-lived and unsuccessful attempt to require a list of candidates from whom to choose the Governor-General rather than simply accept the nomination of Sir Isaac Isaacs – happened more than 60 years ago. British officials (rather than the monarch) also tried to resist the appointment of the

Australian General Sir John Northcott as Governor of NSW in the late 1940s. The last attempt to involve the monarch in Australia's internal politics was actually perpetrated by the Labor Party when the Parliamentary Speaker Gordon Scholes wrote to the Queen requesting her intervention to reverse the dismissal of Gough Whitlam. She declined the invitation, replying through her Private Secretary that all her powers and responsibilities under the Australian Constitution were to be exercised by the Australian Governor-General. As the Turnbull Committee has itself pointed out, the Queen's role under the Australian Constitution is limited to appointing and, if need be, dismissing the Governor-General on the advice of the Australian Prime Minister.

Although many regard 1975 as the *annus horribilis* of the Australian Constitution, it is better understood as an illustration of the powers of the Australian Crown as exercised by the Governor-General. The Queen had nothing to do with it. Republicans usually claim that the dismissal by an unelected governor-general of an elected prime minister with a majority in the House of Representatives was an affront to democracy. Others regard 1975 as a political – rather than a constitutional – crisis in which the Governor-General resolved a political deadlock in the most democratic way possible, with an election by the people deciding the outcome.

The shadow of 1975
The events of 11 November, 1975 raise key issues such as: should a government's budget require approval by the Senate; should a government which cannot pass its budget through both Houses of Parliament be obliged to resign; and should a non-elected person be able to sack a prime minister who continues to hold a majority in the Lower House? These are important bones of

constitutional contention but none of them will be resolved simply by replacing a governor-general with a president.

The events of 1975 illustrate the strengths (rather than any limitations) of the existing system. Although the system of government did not prevent confrontation developing, the pride of the contestants was mostly to blame. Although the Governor-General's intervention could be seen as thwarting the results of the 1974 poll, it allowed democratic principles to assert themselves at the 1975 poll. The system worked. There were no riots in the streets; no political deaths; no acts of civil disobedience; no lasting alienation nor disenfranchisement of anyone. Australia's democracy was tested, not broken. Most importantly, at least in the context of debate over whether to change the constitutional arrangements governing the head of state, 1975 showed that – for all practical purposes – the Governor-General is at the apex of Australia's constitutional structure.

In 1970, when the Labor Party had itself sought to defeat Budget measures, Opposition Leader Whitlam had told Parliament:

> Any government which is defeated by the Parliament on a major taxation bill should resign... This bill will be defeated in another place. The Government should then resign.

In 1967 and again in 1970, the then Labor Leader in the Senate, Lionel Murphy, had declared that:

> There are no limitations on the Senate in the use of its constitutional powers except the limits self-imposed by discretion and reason. There is no tradition in the Australian Labor Party that we will not oppose in the Senate any tax or money bill.

In fact, Murphy then tabled a list of 169 occasions when Labor oppositions had attempted to do what the Coalition did in 1975.

In the different circumstances of 1975, Whitlam claimed otherwise and failed to follow the precedent he had previously set by calling an election in the face of the Senate's 1974 threat to block a revenue bill. Claiming that the Senate had no right to block Budget Bills, he declared that the Government could continue as long as it commanded a majority in the Lower House. What the Government might do when supply voted the previous May ran out was not entirely clear but Whitlam talked about borrowing from the banks to continue to pay public servants and to fund government programmes.

The Constitution omits to state that a prime minister unable to secure the passage of his Budget through the Parliament should resign. This, in fact, is such a basic principle of the Westminster system that our constitutional founders took it for granted. Similarly, they took for granted the equally fundamental Westminster principle (on which the Constitution is similarly silent) that, except in emergencies, the Crown (in Australia's case, the Governor-General) always acts on ministerial advice.

The reserve powers of the Crown

As long as the Prime Minister is entitled to remain in office, the Governor-General is bound to take his advice. The Governor-General's 'reserve powers' only come into play when there is some doubt about the Prime Minister's entitlement to office: for instance, where it appears that the Prime Minister lacks the confidence of the Parliament yet the Parliament is unreasonably prevented from meeting; where the Prime Minister refuses to resign after losing a vote of confidence; or where the Prime Minister cannot secure the passage of the Budget yet refuses to resign.

Hence, on 11 November, 1975, after ascertaining that neither Prime Minister Whitlam nor Opposition Leader Malcolm Fraser would budge from their positions and after obtaining an assurance from Fraser that he would advise an election, Sir John Kerr dismissed Whitlam and appointed Fraser caretaker Prime Minister. Recommending an election was the only substantive action Fraser took during the caretaker period. Although polls showed Fraser's actions in denying supply were unpopular, the subsequent election saw him win the biggest majority in Australia's history and the highest ever percentage of the two-party preferred vote. This was despite the fact that the ALP tried to turn the election into a referendum on the Governor-General's actions.

The circumstances of modern government, with strong party discipline and preferential voting for the Lower House, coupled with a proportionally-elected Senate where governments rarely have a majority, mean that the Senate's ability to force the Government to the people is an important check on executive power. In Victoria, the Upper House twice forced Governments to the polls in the 1950s. Federally, Government Senators crossed the floor to defeat a money bill in 1959 – but the Government re-submitted the bill and it was passed. In 1991, the Opposition threatened to vote against a money bill which retrospectively validated MPs' postal allowances which the High Court said had been used illegally – but, this time, there was no intention to force the Government to an election. The trauma of 1975 means that no Opposition would lightly attempt to block supply. But the power is there to be used again in an extreme situation and the Governor-General would again have the role of resolving the resulting crisis.

If the Governor-General had lacked the power to dismiss a prime minister, the end of 1975 crisis might well have been worse. The political parties were in a state of deadlock. The irresistible force of Whitlam's will had met the immovable object of Fraser's determination. The Prime Minister was proposing to govern in defiance of the Constitution. Perhaps the Senate might have cracked under the pressure and let the supply bills through – but the fact that Opposition Senators had voted to defer consideration of supply three times suggests that such a collapse was unlikely. The appropriations previously authorised by Parliament were on the point of being exhausted and any attempt to govern without supply was a breach of the fundamental principle of constitutional law (established since the time of Edward III and confirmed by the English Civil War) that the executive government cannot raise money from the people without the authorisation of Parliament.

At State level, there have been two recent examples of vice-regal representatives acting in accordance with their own discretion when the ordinary political process has broken down. In 1987, when the Queensland Premier had lost the confidence of his Cabinet but was refusing to resign, Governor Sir Walter Campbell commissioned the new leader of the National Party to form a Government. In 1989, when the Tasmanian Premier lost his majority at an election and his opponents formed a de-facto coalition, Governor Sir Phillip Bennett chose to commission the former Opposition Leader without waiting for a parliamentary vote. Both decisions were ultimately uncontentious – and both demonstrate the role of a detached umpire.

Some republicans (as well as some of their opponents) say that the Governor-General's insecurity of tenure is a serious weakness in our existing system. In fact, the power of the Prime Minister to dismiss the Governor-General, and vice versa, means that each must take the other seriously. But even if this were the important constitutional failing that some republicans claim, it could be resolved through the passage of an Act of Parliament providing that, except in cases of proven misbehaviour or incapacity, the Governor-General shall be appointed for five years. Insecurity of tenure may justify changing the law – but, of itself, hardly justifies becoming a republic. Such a change, of course, would strengthen the Governor-General's hand (in any dispute with the Prime Minister) and to that extent would upset the current constitutional balance.

The concept of the Crown is deeply embedded in the Westminster system because the long struggle between King and Parliament (and subsequently the changing relationship between executive government and Parliament) has given our system its shape. One of the serious complications of any move to a republic is the necessity to transfer formal powers to a president (without losing the existing monarchical conventions against those powers' misuse). No Governor-General, for instance, would dream of actually commanding the armed forces (if only because it would lead to instant dismissal). But a president with a five year term might have very different ideas.

Guardian of the Constitution

The Governor-General's role as guardian of the Constitution is not limited to the type of crisis which might occur once-in-a-lifetime. The Crown's representative has a significant role in the everyday workings of government. The Governor-General chairs the Executive Council which transacts the formal business of government, such as signing regulations into law and making official appointments. This is not a mere formality and a number of vice-regal representatives have described returning matters to the Government for re-consideration, not because of policy disagreements but because of technical deficiencies no-one else had noticed.

The Governor-General's role as 'final proof-reader' of laws and

regulations is a little-appreciated component of the existing checks and balances on executive government. A pamphlet issued while he was in office by the former Governor of Victoria, Richard McGarvie, describes the Governor's role:

> ... to ensure that the powers of Governor-in-Council are exercised regularly so as to be constitutional, valid and effective, in compliance with any principles of natural justice or procedural fairness which apply and in accordance with the appropriate practices and conventions of good government.

McGarvie states that:

> This is the last check on the public service in a process which is often not the subject of other outside surveillance. If it appears that a course proposed for the Governor-in-Council would not be regular, the Governor... has the Clerk seek information or raise questions of the appropriateness of the proposed course with the Department concerned.

In some cases, McGarvie adds:

> The Minister is requested to discuss the matter with the Governor [because] the mark of a good Minister is a desire... that executive powers be exercised regularly.

On the basis of his own experience in Government House, McGarvie observes that:

> Ministers are typically most ready to give full consideration if the Governor counsels that particular action proposed would or might be irregular and to advise a course which they are satisfied will be regular.

Critics described the approach of the former NSW Governor, Admiral Peter Sinclair:

> He has frequently refused to sign Executive Council papers until he has been given more information – a habit described by some ministers as 'bothersome' because his questioning and demands have never led to any decisions being rescinded or revised.

Telegraph, **23 January, 1996**

Sir Paul Hasluck once said that the Governor-General:

> Has the responsibility to weigh and evaluate the advice and has the opportunity of discussion with his ministers. It would be precipitate and probably out of keeping with the nature of his office for him to reject advice outright but he is under no compulsion to accept it unquestioningly...

Quoted by David Smith, *Australian National Review*, **July 1997**

The counsel offered to a government by a governor-general or governor can be confided, if at all, only to the pages of a memoir. It is not surprising that the representative of the Crown is often depicted as a mere opener of flower shows and cutter of ribbons at fetes. But those who have served on the Executive Council of the Commonwealth or a State know that the Crown's role is more than merely formal. In any event, the ceremonial functions that occupy so much vice-regal time are far from trivial. Unlike even the best and most widely respected political leader, the Governor-General has no partisan axe to grind and is well placed, as Sir Zelman Cowen put it, to interpret the nation to itself.

As Cowen has said:

> The many ceremonies, attendances, openings and speeches of the Governor-General are associated with an extremely wide spectrum of activities in the life of the nation, ranging from the broadly national to the local. They take the Governor-General to many places... in a vast continent and they require him to speak on many themes, issues and events, to interpret, to offer suggestions and ideas, to challenge and to encourage... I believe Hasluck was right in saying Australians both expect and appreciate statements by a Governor-General on matters of current or enduring concern at a level different from that of party political controversy, and I was intellectually stretched and tested in preparing for speeches, meetings and activities that called on my knowledge, experiences and capacities.

Australian, **15 June, 1995**

In Australia, the Crown has always had connotations of service as well as authority. The early Governors acknowledged a duty to protect the Aborigines. They failed, of course, but not always from want of trying. In an act indicating at least some Royal concern, Prince Alfred, the first Royal tourist, visited Truganini as well as a settlement at Lake Alexandrina. Detractors may say that these Aborigines were 'Uncle Toms' – but the evidence is against it and the rapturous reception he received suggests that loyalty to the Crown had taken root in unlikely places [Atkinson, p. 8].

To oppose the Government but not the State

The existence of the Crown enables Australia to meet two hard-to-express but important-to-have requirements of government. Successful government needs a human face. If it is to be accepted by the people, government cannot be a huge machine which turns citizens into units of production. Yet even the best government will make mistakes. People need the ability to reject a government without rejecting authority itself. As the embodiment of authority, the Crown is a response to the need to personalise institutions. On the other hand, by separating the concept of the state from the conduct of government, the Crown provides a sphere of national leadership which is uncontaminated by partisan politics.

Perhaps one of the reasons why Australians can mostly take their politicians or leave them (regardless of virtues or vices) is because the Crown helps to keep politicians in their place. Proof that a president could lie and cheat like other politicians seems to have hurt the American psyche. A Watergate-style national anxiety attack is almost impossible to imagine in Australia because politicians have never occupied the highest pedestal in the land – and thus do not have as far to fall!

The mystique of the Crown – and the powerful conventions governing the office – have preserved the Governor-Generalship from political taint even when former politicians have been appointed to the job. Although Justice Kerr's appointment was questioned, ironically enough, because he was supposed to be too close to the Labor Party, the most significant controversy has involved the appointment of former senior politicians: Sir William McKell was Premier of NSW when appointed by Ben Chifley; Lord Casey had been a long-serving Foreign Minister in Menzies' Government – although he had retired prior to appointment as Governor-General; Sir Paul Hasluck was the serving Foreign Minister when John Gorton announced his appointment as Governor-General; as was Bill Hayden when his appointment was announced by Bob Hawke.

Successful governors-general do not need to have been politically neutral in the past. They simply need to be plausible as impartial figures while in office. In prior public life, every Australian governor-general has demonstrated the qualities of intellect, character, and statecraft required by the job. Hence, a suitable governor-general is not necessarily one who has never upset people but one who has the capacity to inspire others plus the moral strength to resist powerful pressures. Governors-general have been politically aware – but not politically active. They have been able to treat with the Prime Minister of the day as an equal, not an underling, and have invariably been bigger, not smaller, characters than the normal run of senior politicians.

CHAPTER THREE

A brief history of
Australian republicanism

REPUBLICANISM is almost as old as Australia itself. There must have been a fair percentage of republicans amongst the Irish convicts – especially those transported after the 1798 rebellion – and the so-called Battle of Vinegar Hill in 1804 had strong Irish overtones.

Although John Dunmore Lang failed to get a seconder when he moved a NSW parliamentary motion calling for 'separation' of the colony from England in 1859, a number of our most prominent 19th century figures were republican in sentiment at least. They included the poet Charles Harpur, the NSW politician E.W. O'Sullivan and the Victorians George Higinbotham and Charles Gavan Duffy – but other instinctive republicans, such as Henry Parkes, came to appreciate the virtues of British institutions (as well as their practical benefits, such as the protection of the Royal Navy). As O'Sullivan put it in 1893:

> I am a republican in theory but there is so little difference between a republic and the limited monarchy of England that it is not worth talking about. The monarchy of England is merely a veiled republic. [see Winterton p. 56]

For 200 years, Australian republicanism waxed and waned

mostly in response to the ups and downs of Australia's relationship with Britain but partly in tune with Australians' self-understandings. Nationalism produced gold rush republicans and federation republicans. Anti-British feeling produced conscription republicans and body-line republicans. Whitlam republicans thought that Australia was standing on its own two feet at last and dismissal republicans thought that the Viceroy was interfering in Australian politics.

Amongst the dismissal republicans were some who thought that the Queen had too much power and others who thought that the Governor-General had too much power. Some, in other words, who were reflecting the old animosity to the 'foreign queen' and others who were starting to focus on the mechanics of the Australian Constitution.

1975 marked something of a watershed. For the first time in our history, people other than judges and professors of law took an interest in Australian constitutional theory. Equally, for the first time in our history, constitutional laymen began to understand that the Governor-General was a rather more important figure under our Constitution than a mere Queen's deputy.

Prior to 1975, republicanism was generally a sentimental abstraction to be argued in the Celtic Club or the RSL bar. It tended to be a question of whether the monarchy could fit Australia's egalitarian nature or Pacific destiny; or whether a republic would betray our cultural identity and institutional foundations. Yet systems of government are founded on reason as well as instinct. The post-1975 discussion of the role of the Senate and the extent of the reserve powers of the Crown began the transformation of the republican debate. It became less a question of tribal passion and more a question of practical politics. It became less focused on issues of identity and more focused on the Constitution itself.

The Bicentenary Constitutional Commission, as part of an exhaustive review, considered whether Australia should become a republic – only to reject it because there was no constituency for change. In June 1991, the Australian Labor Party formally committed itself ('not very vigorously' as Chairman John Bannon observed when the resolution passed on the voices) to achieving a republic by 2001. The Australian Republican Movement, launched a few weeks later, was dedicated to tackling the practicalities of becoming a republic while simultaneously building that constituency for change.

The St Patrick's Day republic

The 'foreign queen' soon had plenty of critics. With Tom Keneally stirring up the 'children of Ireland' (going over the top at a St Patrick's Day bash to the extent of likening the Queen to a colostomy bag on the Australian body politic) and with large numbers of post-war migrants lacking any affinity for Britain, it was not hard to project the 'Queen of England' as a parasite in the Australian system.

It was one thing, however, to score cheap points at the expense of the Royal Family but quite another to persuade people to change Australia's system of government. Before very long, the republican movement was trying to argue that there was nothing essentially wrong with our system of government – yet the Constitution should be substantially re-written in order to make a symbolic change.

The fact that the republican movement was able to attract prominent Australians such as Keneally, author Donald Horne, historian John Hirst and lawyers George Winterton and Malcolm Turnbull showed how the standing of the Crown had diminished in a generation. Yet Turnbull, Winterton, and Hirst (who each published draft republican constitutions) could only agree on the broad shape (and not the detail) of an Australian republic and no republican (aside from Keating while he was Prime Minister) had the authority to exercise national leadership.

A significant landmark was the publication, in September 1991, of Hirst's essay 'The Conservative Case for an Australian Republic'. Australians had stopped singing *God Save The Queen* at the pictures, given up toasting the Queen as a matter of course at every civic banquet, removed the monarch's name from citizenship oaths, erased the crown from post boxes and no longer reverently opened Government envelopes adorned with the letters 'OHMS' (On Her Majesty's Service). The monarch was no longer a mythic presence in Australian life, said Hirst, and had irredeemably lost her civic personality.

It was a fair point – except that Catholic school essays have similarly lost their dedication 'AMDG' (to the greater glory of God) without anyone (on that ground) calling for their abolition. This is the age of irreverence. Church, parliament, courts and police have lost respect just as fast as the Crown. The challenge, of course, is to make these institutions work rather than dump them and start again. Hirst's article, coming as it did from a key conservative historian, was important because it was a sign of constitutional apathy among the Crown's natural defenders.

In January 1992, freshly installed as Prime Minister, Paul Keating began to create a new image for himself with an attack on the Australian Flag. As Treasurer, Keating had implemented major economic changes. However, financial deregulation and the 'internationalisation' of the economy had created losers as well as winners – many of whom were part of Labor's traditional constituency. Prime Minister Keating needed an issue to win back Labor supporters alienated by Treasurer Keating and, in particular, to deflect the hostility of the Labor left born in

NSW factional wars and recently honed in the struggle to oust Bob Hawke.

Symbols of sovereignty

Observers such as Hugh Stretton detected a paradox in the Keating Government's determination to assert Australian sovereignty over the Constitution (which was never in doubt) at the same time as the Government was cheerfully relinquishing sovereignty over the economy. For the ALP left, however, republicanism became a totem of the Keating Government's commitment to something other than textbook-inspired economic policies.

In February 1992, at a Parliament House reception for the Queen, Keating made a speech emphasising that Britain and Australia were going their separate ways. The over-reaction of some Liberals, who accused Keating of lacking manners, prompted a furious assault in Parliament. Keating savaged the British for abandoning 'Malaysia' (sic) in 1942 and sacrificing 15,000 Australians (conveniently forgetting the 100,000 British and Empire troops who shared their fate). For good measure, he excoriated Liberal leaders John Hewson and John Howard as belonging in a museum of the '50s, seeking imperial honours as a substitute for standing up for Australia.

'Annus horribilis' is how the Queen described 1992. It was the year Prince Charles announced his separation and when Royal scuttlebutt became a media staple. 'Royalty' became associated with spoilt Sloane Rangers having their toes sucked by 'financial advisers'. And when Keating described Australia to an Indonesian audience as virtually the last outpost of the British Empire and told a PNG child waving an Australian Flag that he would 'get him a new one soon', the political opposition was mostly too preoccupied with selling a new tax to contest the matter.

Donald Horne had written that, when the time came,

republicans would find themselves pushing 'on a door lightly locked'. Still, the republican movement had problems of its own. Horne's book, *The Coming Republic*, juxtaposed serious analysis with an imaginary party, in which an Australian republic was the triumphant conclusion of a long lunch. Keneally's announcement that Blinky Bill had been recruited as the republican mascot was unfortunate – especially as it was the Hollywood version and not Dorothy Wall's original that was chosen.

In June 1992, an anti-republican organisation, Australians for Constitutional Monarchy, was established under the motto: 'Defend the Constitution'. ACM was the brainchild of two Sydney lawyers: Michael Kirby, law reformer (and subsequently High Court judge), who insisted that ACM pitch its message beyond the 'old white conservatives' often caricatured as the Crown's only supporters; and Lloyd Waddy, senior barrister and chairman of the Australian Elizabethan Theatre Trust, who acted as spokesman and organiser.

Kirby and Waddy had two objectives: to ensure that debate focused on the Constitution rather than the Royal Family; and to see that the Constitution's defenders reflected the diversity of modern Australia. Kirby drafted a Charter of Australians for Constitutional Monarchy which embraced everyone from ardent royalists, to strong constitutionalists, to republicans who were in no hurry for change. With Waddy, he set about recruiting prominent citizens to spearhead a campaign to defend the Constitution by becoming members of ACM's Foundation Charter Council.

Key members of the Foundation Charter Council included Sydney University Chancellor Dame Leonie Kramer and ex-High Court Chief Justice Sir Harry Gibbs (to provide academic and legal expertise), former Aboriginal Senator Neville Bonner and

Chinese-born NSW MP Helen Sham-Ho (to provide ethnic balance) and former Labor Lord Mayor of Sydney Doug Sutherland (to demon-strate political neutrality). Kirby's presence was crucial because it demonstrated that support for the Crown was not limited to members of the intellectual right.

Nevertheless, the public launch of ACM, on 4 June, 1992, was reported in terms of elderly ladies lustily singing *God Save the Queen*. The West Australian Labor maverick Graeme Campbell subsequently sent up media prejudices, telling a full-house rally in the main Sydney Town Hall that 'tomorrow's papers will say there was only 200 here and we were all over 90'.

In 1992, the one eventuality that looked more certain than the end of the monarchy in Australia was the defeat of the Keating Government. Had Keating lost the 1993 election, republicanism would have been largely forgotten (at least by headline writers) in the attempt to come to terms with the Fightback! programme. In fact, the re-elected Keating Government's first significant act was to appoint a Republic Advisory Committee to advise on how such a change might be achieved.

Although Liberal leader John Hewson (narrowly re-elected as party leader after defeat in the 'unloseable' 1993 election) had just described 'hard-line monarchists' as 'out of touch', he refused to appoint a representative to the Republic Advisory Committee on the grounds that the party's policy was to support the Constitution as it stood. Keating invited the State Premiers to nominate members – and proceeded to choose a relatively junior Sydney solicitor (nominated by NSW Premier John Fahey) ahead of Victorian Premier Jeff Kennett's nomination, Australia's foremost historian, Geoffrey Blainey.

The key members of the Committee were Chairman Malcolm Turnbull (who was also chairman of the Australian Republican

Movement), John Hirst and George Winterton (who were also prominent members of the ARM) and former NSW Liberal Premier Nick Greiner (also a declared republican, who was selected in a bid for bi-partisan support). The Committee's brief was to advise on ways of becoming a republic and part of its task was to travel round the country gauging public opinion.

Republic advocacy committee

Critics said that the $600,000 Committee budget amounted to taxpayer support for one side of the argument. To ensure even-handedness, they said, the Government would need to appoint a 'monarchy advisory committee' headed by Lloyd Waddy and including Leonie Kramer and Harry Gibbs with the same budget and the same job of roaming the country taking soundings.

As an exercise in popular democracy, the Turnbull Committee was a failure. Twenty-two separate public meetings around the country attracted just 1,500 people. At the largest meetings, in Sydney and Canberra, majorities were hostile to the Committee's pro-republican speakers. Other meetings attracted a derisory turnout. Government figures showed that just four people attended a public meeting in Kalgoorlie and five in Port Hedland while the local paper claimed that just one local person had turned up in Whyalla [*Whyalla News*, 9 July, 1993]. Committee member George Winterton later admitted his surprise at the popular response which was 'either strongly royalist or against the Keating republic' [*Sydney Morning Herald*, 8 September, 1993].

When released in October 1993, the Committee's report of 150 pages plus 340 pages of appendices failed to answer the basic question: why should Australia become a republic in the first place? Committee members argued that it was not within their terms of reference and that the desirability of becoming a republic would depend upon the republican options available.

Yet the Committee's decision not to make a case for becoming a republic enabled critics to say that the whole debate was meaningless: like arguing about how to get to Newcastle before there was any need or desire to go.

Moreover, the Report made three important concessions to anti-republicans. First (because Australia is a monarchy in each State as well as the Commonwealth) the Report conceded that some States could remain monarchies in any Federal republic – a result which was described as a 'constitutional monstrosity' [Report, p. 128]. Second, although the Report concluded (on the basis of an opinion from the Government's Acting Solicitor-General) that a majority of the people in a majority of the States could actually over-rule the State Constitutions, it conceded political force in the argument that this could unravel the whole Federal compact [Report, p. 130]. Third, it dismissed the 'Tippex' option (substituting 'president' for 'governor-general' in the existing Constitution) as having the potential for autocracy [Report, p. 116].

This was an important concession by the Report's republican authors and reinforced earlier concerns that giving the Governor-General's existing powers to a virtually unsackable president contained the seeds of a possible future dictatorship.

The association in the public's mind between constitutional change and an increasingly arrogant Prime Minister marred the Report's reception. Keating's legendary description of the Senate as 'unrepresentative swill' and of Question Time as a 'privilege' extended by the Executive to the Parliament exemplified his indifference to constitutional niceties whenever they got in his way. On the day the Turnbull Report was released, the Prime Minister walked out of parliamentary Question Time after 15 minutes because he did not like the tenor of proceedings.

Meanwhile, the 'inevitable' republic had tripped on the opinion polls. In April 1993, Newspoll recorded 46% support for a republic and 39% opposition. In September, it almost exactly reversed and stayed that way until January 1995 when it again showed nearly 50% supporting and 40% opposing a republic. Although opposition to a republic (as measured by Newspoll) fell to just 29% in April 1997, support only exceeded 50% in the emotionally charged anti-Royal atmosphere after Princess Diana's death.

In the wake of Sydney winning the 2000 Olympics, Keating briefly brought forward his republican target date – on the grounds that it would be unthinkable for a 'foreign' Queen to open the Australian Olympics. However, others suggested that it was equally unthinkable for Australia to change its constitution for the sake of a sporting event.

At the same time, pollsters were starting to ask more sophist-icated questions. In particular, they began asking, 'if a republic were to occur, how should the president be elected?', and 'would you support a republic if the president was not elected?'. A clear message from these more discriminating questions was that – if Australia were to become a republic – about four fifths of the people would want to elect their own president. So far at least, only about 40% would support a republic against the existing system if the president was to be elected by politicians rather than the people.

Ever since republicanism became front page news, the Liberal Party has been plagued by 'split' stories. John Hewson's focus was predominantly economic and, after the ALP's initial decision to opt for a republic, he claimed that the Liberal Party did not have a policy on the subject – even though, close to his own portrait in the Coalition party room in Canberra, was a statement of Liberal principles signed by Bob Menzies beginning 'we believe in the Crown'.

Until 1994, everyone joining the Liberal Party in NSW did so on a form including the statement 'we believe... in the constitutional monarchy' ranked above 'we believe... in a just and humane society' in a statement of Liberal principles. Hewson went to the 1993 election tepidly endorsing the Constitution, more warmly embracing the Flag but mostly insisting that the whole issue was a Keating-inspired diversion from Australia's economic problems.

In September 1993, the Federal Council of the Liberal Party re-considered its attitude and decided that, while keeping an open mind about the future, in the absence of much better arguments for change, Liberals backed the Constitution we had. Every State conference carried motions supporting the Constitution and rejecting republicanism. One pro-republican Liberal described the:

> Catcalls of 'traitor' and 'wrecker'... as I stood to commence my speech... As I sat down... I was jostled and abused by angry party members.
>
> *Australian*, **13 June, 1995**

Nick Greiner's support for a republic, and his successor John Fahey's statement that a republic was inevitable, made the NSW Liberal Party seem much more republican than it really was. Little noticed, thanks to the ALP's tighter discipline over serving MPs and the media's focus on change, was Bob Hawke's comment that 'monarchists are winning the intellectual battle' and Bill Hayden's statement that our existing system 'works well'. The reluctance of Labor's elder statesmen to back the Keating crusade seemed to confirm poll results suggesting that there were almost as many Labor-voting monarchists as Liberal-voting republicans.

In October 1995, while still serving as Governor-General,

Hayden said that he was neither monarchist nor republican but that he preferred 'to support what works best'.

> There are some very serious pitfalls in becoming a republic, [which republicans had to fix] so we don't run into trouble later... We need to be sure if we do anything that it is workable and doesn't have serious defects – it doesn't cause greater problems than it is proposed to solve.
>
> *Sydney Morning Herald,* **26 October, 1995**

Change the Flag too?

In June 1994, Keating officially declared a truce in his campaign to change the Flag after Labor officials insisted it was a vote-loser and Finance Minister Kim Beazley had pointedly said that the flag issue was 'the Prime Minister's baby'. Keating told journalists that he had 'an opinion on the flag but not a plan for the flag' [*Australian* 15 June, 1994]. But throughout his term, he refused to fly the Australian Flag on his official car and said he wanted to return to this issue if a republic was achieved [*Sydney Morning Herald*, 26 April, 1993].

At the same time, ARM Chairman Turnbull resigned his directorship of the change-the-Flag organisation, Ausflag, because it was confusing the message of the republican push (although there is little evidence that he had changed his mind or his objectives). In February 1996, for instance, an exhibit 'Flagging the Republic' (featuring more than 70 designs for a new flag including one entitled 'fuck off back to fagland') was sponsored by Turnbull's merchant bank.

In July 1994, with a new Liberal leader at the helm, the republicans executed a media 'hit' designed to highlight their opponents' difficulties. Because no referendum could succeed without bi-partisan support, the republicans' tactic was to try to 'spook' Liberal leaders into joining a bandwagon. Thus, every Liberal who could be persuaded to 'come out' as a republican was both a tactical advance and a psychological win putting pressure on more conservative-minded colleagues.

One Sunday, the ARM announced the appointment of a new Vice-President, John Fahey-staffer (now Senator) Marise Payne. The next day, Hewson-staffer Andrew Parker announced the existence of a secret 'new republic' cell inside the Liberal Party dedicated to overturning the Party's traditional position (about which no evidence, apart from Parker's statement, was ever produced). Two days later, republican sources re-announced as supporters those Liberal politicians who had already gone on-the-record as critics of the party's traditional view. In response, Liberal Leader Alexander Downer first dismissed the unrest as the work of 'mere staffers' but ended up claiming that the Queen was seen as 'a quaint Englishwoman' who was 'irrelevant' to the Australian constitutional debate.

Downer's eventual decision to call for a people's convention in 1997, to mark the centenary of the Adelaide Convention at which our Constitution took its final shape, was a deft escape from a no-win situation. He added that the Convention should consider the reach of the Federal Government's powers and the question of waste and duplication between the various levels of Government as well as the role of the head of state.

Downer's decision wrapped high principle in smart politics. Republicans were assured that they would have the chance to argue their case when the time came. Anti-republicans took comfort from the party's continued support for the Crown. And everyone could accept that, if change should come, it must be shaped by the people rather than by the Prime Minister.

But not, republicans insisted, by Australians who happened to have been born in Britain and to have gone on the electoral roll prior to 1984 (when the Citizenship Act was changed) without actually becoming Australian citizens. In September 1997, just prior to the Convention ballot, Ausflag reportedly backed a High Court challenge to the right of un-naturalised British citizens to vote in the postal ballot. Turnbull commented that if people think

> ... so little about Australia that, being entitled to become citizens, they have chosen not to be one, then you would have to ask how they could in good conscience vote for this Constitutional Convention.

Australian Financial Review, **15 September, 1997**

A curious feature of the debate was Keating's preference for lecturing overseas audiences about his plans to shake off Australia's colonial image. He told the French President of his plans for a republic after visiting Napoleon's Palace. He told the German Chancellor of his republican aspirations before visiting the birthplace of George III. In March 1995, he praised Germany's 'appointed' presidency (even though the German President is actually chosen by an absolute majority of MPs). His claims that the German President is 'not a member of a political party' and 'not a political figure' – even though the current President is a member of the Christian Democrat Union and, like all his predecessors, retains his party political affiliation, showed an unusual definition of non-partisanship (*AM,* 8 March, 1995).

Although the Keating Government had not planned to vote on the subject until at least 1997, it embarked on a campaign of petty or creeping republicanism. As Prime Minister, Keating changed the ministerial oath of office so that Government Ministers did not swear allegiance to the Crown. John Howard restored the practice of Ministers swearing allegiance to the Queen (although not to her 'heirs and successors'). Thanks to Keating, new migrants no longer take an oath of allegiance to the Queen (although the new 'user-friendly' citizenship pledge is arguably a stylistic improvement on the old legalistic oath). Under Keating, Government bookshops did not sell the Queen's photograph, which was also removed from most government offices and Australian embassies.

Meanwhile, the republican movement remained much better at attracting publicity than members. In November 1993, the ARM launched a strategy designed to attract a grassroots membership of 50,000 [*Time,* 15 November, 1993]. In July 1994, the ARM's communications adviser claimed 5,000 members. But, in a debate in May 1995, Executive Director Michael Ward said that membership was 4,000 – which was the same number as claimed two years earlier. Early in 1997, the ARM claimed 6,000 members [*Australian Financial Review,* 7 April, 1997] – even though, some months earlier, it had reportedly been unable to afford the services of its three full-time staff [*Australian,* 11 May, 1996].

Sydney chardonnay republicans

In late 1994, after the announcement that he had agreed to become a republican 'ambassador', football coach Ron Barassi said that becoming a republic 'won't make a big difference', was not worth 'spending a lot of time on' and was 'not important enough to be divisive about' [*AM,* 24 October, 1994]. Kate Ceberano denied that she had agreed to become an 'ambassador' and other 'ambassadors' did not want to discuss their involvement with the ARM. One report said that some ARM members were unhappy with the 'Sydney dinner party republicans' running the show [*Sun-Herald,* 21 May, 1995]. Another dissenting report claimed that ARM supporters resented Turnbull's 'brash, egocentric, sometimes overbearing, sometimes bullying personal style' [*Australian,* 9 October, 1995].

By contrast, in April 1995, after organisers of a Canberra arts festival displayed a nude statue of the Queen and Prince Phillip, Australians for Constitutional Monarchy signed up their 12,000th supporter. In January 1996, after NSW Premier Bob Carr's attempt to close Government House and introduce a part-time Governor, ACM organised a march on Parliament House of up to 20,000 protesters and enrolled their 17,000th supporter.

Carr's maladroit attempt to vindicate the memory of Jack Lang caused serious tensions inside the ALP. 'He gave a spirited defence of his actions but not a lot of us were sold on it' said one MP. 'There was a general feeling that he'd handled it badly' [*Telegraph*, 8 February, 1996]. A Federal Labor MP, Mary Easson, even wrote to the 'Friends of Government House' saying that 'personally, I am in favour of a Governor' and that 'this matter will settle down in a way that leads to a continuation of the normal procedures involving the Governor of NSW and Government House'. As it turned out, the establishment of a non-resident Governor saved just $80,000 (with costs falling from $2.73 million to $2.65 million) in the first year of operation [*Telegraph*, 25 August, 1997].

Originally, the Keating Government had said it would respond to the Turnbull Report within a year. In October 1994, the Prime Minister said that 'pressures of work' had made it difficult to concentrate on such an 'esoteric' subject [*Australian*, 8 October, 1994]. In March 1995, Government sources described the announcement as 'imminent' [*Australian*, 22 March, 1995]. It was postponed again in the wake of the disastrous Canberra by-election. After Turnbull accused the Government of 'wimping out', the announcement was re-scheduled as a parliamentary statement on Wednesday 7 June, 1995.

When finally unveiled, the Keating republic entailed a president elected by a two thirds majority of both Houses of Parliament exercising, it was claimed, much the same powers as the Governor-General does now. A curious feature of the Keating republic was his desire to replace a system supported (polls said) by more-or-less a third of the Australian people with one opposed by more-or-less three quarters of the Australian people. Not only did Keating reject the option of a president elected by the people (despite the overwhelming opinion poll support for popular election), he also rejected the idea of a popularly elected convention to formulate a draft republican constitution (even though this was the procedure followed during the federation era to turn a collection of colonies into a nation).

Keating's republic was the culmination of a three year political strategy designed to maximise the chance of success by minimising the appearance of change. He posed the question: 'do you – or don't you – believe in an Australian head of state?' before declaring that our head of state should be 'one of us'. Even Donald Horne subsequently described this is as a 'trick question' [*Australian*, 17 February, 1996] and the fact that Newspoll subsequently recorded 80% for – and only 10% against – an 'Australian head of state' (at a time when support for a republic was under 50%) strongly suggests that the question was meaningless [*Australian*, 21 February, 1996].

The Keating statement should have been a moment of extreme political vulnerability. The end of the long phoney war should have meant that supporters of the Australian Constitution were finally spared the distraction of defending the House of Windsor and could at last begin the much easier task of attacking a virtually unsackable president, unconstrained by conventions, elected by politicians and armed with the Governor-General's existing powers.

Instead, Keating's reception was euphoric. Christine Wallace later described her article for the *Financial Review* (which appeared under the headline, Keating's 'brilliant republican play'), as 'refulgent in its praise' [*Australian Financial Review*,

26 June, 1995]. The reaction to Howard's speech-in-reply could not have been a greater contrast. A typical comment was Alan Ramsey's claim that it was Howard's worst time since the day he first lost the Liberal leadership. Ramsey said:

> This time, he may well have lost the next election and deservedly so. His speech… was that dreadful. It was facile, contrived, pedestrian and disingenuous… It exposed him more brutally than ever as a leader locked into the past, as a politician of indecision, of no courage, no guile, no ideas, no true understanding of his own country in the 1990s and no feel for the future.

Sydney Morning Herald, **10 June, 1995**

The Australian had a front page banner headline: 'Howard avoids the question' [9 June, 1995].

Indeed, the readiness of senior journalists to take sides has been a noteworthy feature of the debate. Paul Kelly, Laurie Oakes, Geoffrey Barker, and Gerard Henderson are among those to have taken an avowedly republican stance – and the most persistent media critic of 'wombat republicanism', Paddy McGuinness, has never been a monarchist.

Nevertheless, in the wake of Keating's republican speech the percentage telling Liberal pollsters that Keating was 'smug, out-of-touch and complacent' jumped 15 points (as reported in Pamela Williams' book, *The Victory*). This was the biggest jump on record in response to a descriptor question and prompted Andrew Robb to tell Howard that voters saw Keating's speech as pompous and arrogant even if journalists did not.

Media boosting

Despite media boosting, republicanism has consistently showed more potential to excite elites than to arouse the average voter. An AGB McNair poll – taken the night after Keating's speech – showed support for a republic down a point to 51%. In three

States – New South Wales, Western Australia and South Australia – support was under 50%. Moreover, only 39% were prepared to support – and 45% opposed – a republic where the head of state was not elected by a vote of the Australian people. The same poll showed that just 32% approved – and 57% disapproved of Parliament electing a president, while 79% approved – and just 17% disapproved – of the people choosing a president by popular vote [*Sydney Morning Herald*, 10 June, 1995].

The night of Howard's statement-in-reply, 12,000 callers in a Channel Seven phone-in poll registered 70% opposition to the Keating plan and over 4000 responses to a *Herald-Sun* 'Vote Line' showed 81% support for the monarchy [*Herald-Sun* 9 June, 1995]. A Newspoll taken a week after both statements showed support for the concept of a republic up 3% (but still only to 50%) and 74% support, should Australia become a republic, for popular election of the head of state. Notwithstanding the barracking of the Canberra Press Gallery, John Howard's option of debating possible change through a constitutional convention scored 2% more support than Paul Keating's [*Australian*, 22 June, 1995].

In his reply, Howard re-affirmed the Coalition's support for a people's convention in 1997. This convention, half-elected and half-appointed and with appointees chosen to give young people and minorities a say, would consider questions such as possible misuse of the foreign affairs power and four year terms for Federal Parliament as well as the head of state. If a consensus emerged, said Howard, he would put it to the people at a referendum.

Howard said that the essential difference between Labor and the Coalition was that 'John Howard would give the Australian people the Constitution they want while Paul Keating would give them the republic he wants'. In effect, he accused Keating of suffering from 'change disease' and of refusing to trust the people – except as part of a cheer squad for the Great Leader. He suggested that Keating regarded his prime ministership as a kind of Year Zero in Australia's history – before which nothing worthwhile really happened, unless it prefigured his own exploits – and contrasted himself as a leader unembarrassed about Australia's past and ready to face up to its future whichever way the Australian people might decide.

In the aftermath of Keating's statement, Queensland Labor Premier Wayne Goss said that politicians should now leave the debate. The Victorian Labor Leader John Brumby said that he preferred to elect a president. But Victorian Liberal Premier Jeff Kennett, hitherto a staunch monarchist, said that Howard's people's convention was 'just another committee'. The Tasmanian and South Australian Liberal Premiers said that a republic was inevitable and proposed State-wide referenda of their own (despite the folly of State-by-State constitutional change).

Three days after delivering his formal response, Howard dropped the Coalition's previous reservation of its right to campaign against the outcome of the Convention and declared that a Coalition Government would promote change, if that were the Convention consensus. Howard said that he would put the issue of the head of state to a vote at an 'indicative plebiscite' regardless of the outcome of the Convention – because the form and substance of change should be settled by the people rather than the Prime Minister. Regardless of the outcome of the 1996 election, he promised, sometime before the turn of the century, Australians would be voting on whether to delete the Crown from the Australian Constitution.

Howard stressed that his support for the Crown was 'personal' rather than 'official'. Effectively, he de-coupled the Liberal Party from the monarchy. As of June 8, 1995, the Liberal Party ceased to be a monarchist party – while maintaining its scepticism about a republic and keeping an open mind on constitutional reform.

Donald Horne once mused that:

> If the good fairy of political causes was to wave her wand over Mr Keating one night, when he was nodding off over a Mahler CD, she would place in his mind the idea, perhaps during one of the trumpet fanfares, that he should announce to his fellow citizens... that it's now up to them to take over the discussion. Once the republic ceases to be 'Keating's republic', the greatest source of opposition to it will fall apart.

> *Sydney Morning Herald,* **3 June, 1995**

Yet, as Keating himself once said, before he took up the cause, 'the republic was something people talked about over the after-dinner mints'. Republicanism may yet turn out to be Keating's bequest to the nation but, in any event, is certainly the biggest item of unfinished business left for John Howard to deal with.

CHAPTER FOUR

The people's convention

INITIALLY, the idea of a people's convention was Alexander Downer's response to an internal Liberal Party problem. The convention option meant that Keating and his 'you'll get the constitution I decide' republic could become the common target of both republicans and monarchists within the Liberal Party.

Although republicanism had never rated highly as a key issue in voter surveys, perceptions of disunity could have damaged the Coalition in the run-up to the 1996 poll. A 1993 survey of the Liberal Party's branch presidents, secretaries and treasurers in Queensland, Western Australia and South Australia found that less than 8% were committed republicans. A survey of the Mosman Young Liberals (one of the biggest Young Liberal branches in Sydney) showed (much to its president's surprise), 67% support for the monarchy. In 1994, 338 Liberal Party branches responding to a party survey said that migrants should swear allegiance to the Queen – and only 157 agreed with dropping her from the citizenship pledge [*Australian,* 21 December, 1994]. In 1997, a repeat survey of Liberal Party branch officials in Queensland showed that only 15% were committed republicans.

In June 1993, more than 50% of Federal Liberal MPs told the *Sydney Morning Herald* that they backed the existing Constitution.

Even 'off-the-record', only three MPs were prepared to back a republic [*Sydney Morning Herald,* 5 June, 1993]. By June 1995, of the 27 Liberal MPs contacted by *The Age* in the wake of both Keating and Howard's statements, five thought that Australia would be a republic by 2001, nine thought that change would come later, seven were relaxed about change and six supported the existing system of Government [*The Age,* 19 June, 1995].

In early 1997, a Sydney newspaper asked all Liberal MPs where they stood on the constitutional question. Seven said they supported a republic, 14 said they supported the existing system and 83 declined to say (on the suggestion of the Chief Whip's office) [*Telegraph,* 24 February, 1997]. This may actually have been a reasonable reflection of party opinion: a handful of dedicated republicans, a somewhat larger group of strong monarchists and a majority with opinions either way but mostly anxious to manage the issue to the Government's benefit.

The same survey recorded just one National Party MP in favour of a republic – although there have been other media claims that up to eight Federal National Party MPs (out of 24) are republicans [*Australian Financial Review*, 3 March, 1997]. In March 1997, the Nationals' Federal Council (according to its subsequent policy newsletter) 'unanimously' supported Australia remaining a constitutional monarchy.

At a Coalition joint party meeting not long after the March '96 election – called specifically to discuss how the Convention policy might work – a number of Federal MPs said that republicanism was not an electoral issue and that the Convention should be dropped. 'If we must have a convention', said one, 'let's hold it at 10pm on Christmas Eve'. Others thought that the Convention would become an expensive talk-fest that solved nothing and that the Government should move straight to an 'indicative plebiscite' pitching a specific republican alternative against the existing Constitution.

Talk-fest followed by an opinion poll

Opinion on the merits of the Convention did not divide on neat pro- and anti-republic lines. Some republicans supported a convention because it would give them an unprecedented opportunity to attack the 'foreign Queen'. Some anti-republicans supported a convention because they saw it as a chance to highlight the difficulties of constitutional change. Others of both constitutional colours believed that – regardless of its ultimate outcome – a proposal for change of this magnitude needed to be thoroughly talked through (and through and through).

On the other hand, different protagonists (on both sides) wanted the argument settled – one way or the other – by a decisive vote of the Australian people. But what would the question be? Turnbull wrote to Coalition MPs calling for the Convention to be replaced by a plebiscite on the question:

> As a matter of principle, would you favour a change to our Constitution to allow an Australian citizen to be our head of state or do you favour the retention of our existing arrangements with the King or Queen of Great Britain remaining our head of state?

Republicans argued that the question: 'Do you want to replace the Governor-General with a president elected by the politicians?' failed to do justice to the range of options for change. Anti-republicans counter-claimed that: 'Do you want an Australian head of state?' was a loaded and misleading question and that conducting a 'multiple choice' plebiscite (with a number of republican alternatives to the existing system) would unfairly maximise opposition to the existing system.

Ultimately, becoming a republic requires a referendum asking voters to opt 'yes' or 'no' to a specific constitutional change.

Moving straight to a referendum was another option. Former Howard adviser Christopher Pearson [*Sydney Morning Herald,* 3 February, 1997] suggested inviting republican MPs to propose a private member's bill to change the Constitution. This, he said, would 'short-circuit' what he described as a 'talk-fest followed by an opinion poll'. The Prime Minister, he said, could announce that he would vote in favour of such a bill – not because he supported a republic – but because he supported putting the matter to a vote. The Government could provide parliamentary time for the matter to be debated and voted upon (along the lines of the procedure adopted for the anti-euthanasia bill) and the Australian people could then pass their verdict on the 'least worst' republican option.

The Pearson proposition had the advantage of facilitating informed constitutional debate, preserving Parliament's role as (if needs be) a standing people's constitutional convention, and resolving the issue in a way which did justice to both sides of the argument. On the other hand, asking Parliament to debate a constitutional referendum (rather than a mere convention) might have meant enormous disruption to the rest of the Government's legislative programme. Senior Government figures worried that parliamentary passage of such a bill (even if only to put the issue decisively to the people) could be portrayed as endorsement of becoming a republic.

It became apparent that simply establishing the form a plebiscite question could take (let alone drafting a bill providing for a constitutional referendum on the establishment of a republic) might itself require the authority of a constitutional convention. The Prime Minister was particularly concerned about rushing Australians into a decision. So after a year of mostly behind-the-scenes talk, in March 1997, he recommitted the Government to a policy which frustrated the impatient on both sides.

The cost of the Convention worried many Coalition MPs. A common view was that $50 million to hold an election for delegates to a convention was an extravagance at a time when the Government was trying to fill the $10 billion 'Beazley budget black hole'. Others said that democracy does not come cheap and that it was worth spending the money to get a new constitution right. Some said that State Parliaments should 'elect' delegates. Others countered that this would produce a 'premiers' convention' rather than a 'people's convention'. In December 1996, Senator Nick Minchin – the Prime Minister's Parliamentary Secretary (subsequently Special Minister of State) with responsibility for constitutional issues – floated the idea of asking local councils to choose delegates to the Convention. Eventually, a compromise was struck: there would be a national, non-compulsory postal ballot for half the delegates, costing about $35 million (or 70% of a standard general election run through polling booths across the nation on a single day).

The size of the Convention was another contentious issue. A big convention would need to be stage-managed. A small convention could hardly pass muster as a national conclave. At the 1897 Convention, each colony was equally represented. Given that the existing Constitution was, in some senses at least, a compact between the States, some MPs argued for equal numbers of delegates from each State. Others argued for 'one vote, one value' across the nation.

In the end, a 'weighting' system was decided upon: there would be 76 elected delegates (the same number as the Senate) and each State would elect delegates in proportion to its representation in the whole Parliament. Because the 76 elected delegates constituted just over one third of the total number of Federal MPs, the delegate numbers from each state would be about a third of a State's total representation in the Federal Parliament. For instance, Tasmania would elect six delegates (because there are 17 Federal MPs elected from Tasmania – five in the House of Representatives and 12 in the Senate). NSW should have elected 21 delegates (because it has 62 MPs in the federal Parliament – 50 MHRs and 12 Senators) but lost a delegate to ensure that the NT elected two. The formula produced 20 delegates from NSW, 16 from Victoria, 13 from Queensland, nine from Western Australia, eight from South Australia, six from Tasmania and two each from the Territories.

In addition to the 76 elected delegates, there were to be 76 appointed delegates: 36 chosen by the Government to 'ensure groups that might not otherwise be adequately represented are afforded the opportunity to participate' (such as people under 25, Aborigines and representatives of local government); 12 delegates chosen by the Federal Coalition; six chosen by the Federal Opposition; one chosen by the Australian Democrats; one chosen from among the Federal Parliamentary independents; three delegates from each of the six State Parliaments (the Premier, Leader of the Opposition and one other) and the two Territory Chief Ministers.

Even with every candidate required to lodge a fee of $500, the Government was concerned that there could be hundreds of nominations in each State producing a ballot paper a metre wide. Under the standard Senate system of voting, this could produce a high percentage of informal votes and a count that took months to complete. Given that less than 5% of Senate voters number every square (while the rest merely put a tick in one party or candidate's box and vote according to the registered preferences of that particular party or candidate), the Government's initial preference was to allow only 'above the line' voting.

But some Government MPs felt that voters might prefer to 'split tickets' adding (say) Donald Horne to an otherwise monarchist ticket or Doug Sutherland to an otherwise republican ticket. Hence the Government decided to allow exhaustive preferential voting for people voting 'above the line' according to registered tickets – and a form of 'first past the post' voting for those who wanted to vote 'below the line' for as many individual candidates as there were positions to be filled.

As well as supplying each voter with 600 word 'yes' and 'no' cases for changing the head of state (cases which would be prepared with the help of the Australian Republican Movement and Australians for Constitutional Monarchy), the Government would provide an election booklet detailing all the various 'tickets' and including a 25 word description of each candidate. In NSW, for instance, voters might cast their ballots 'above the line' for the 'Doug Sutherland – No Republic' ticket or the 'Malcolm Turnbull – Republic by 2001' ticket – or they could vote 'below the line' for individuals by writing down the allocated numbers of the 20 specific candidates for whom they wished to vote. Apart from the leaders of the ticket, no other names would appear on the ballot paper itself, lest it become too big and unwieldy to handle.

Under the Government's original timetable, nominations for elected delegate positions were to close in early July, ballot papers would be in every home by early August, the vote would close in early September, the result would be known by late November and the Convention would deliberate for up to two weeks in early December. As it turned out, the Senate did not finalise its initial consideration of the people's convention legislation until the last week in June.

Voluntary voting

Although he had always preferred to move directly to a plebiscite, Opposition Leader Kim Beazley had originally said that Labor would not oppose the Government's Bill. However, when the Bill came before the Senate in late June, it was rejected twice on the grounds of opposition to voluntary voting. The ALP, Democrats and Senate independents took the view that a non-compulsory vote (coupled with Senator Minchin's long-held public advocacy of voluntary voting) meant that the Convention ballot was a 'Trojan horse' for the general introduction of voluntary voting. However, as Michelle Grattan commented, scuttling any vote at all seemed a strange way to assert the principle of compulsory voting – and the suspicion grew that republicans had wimped out of their first real fight.

The Government insisted that the special circumstances of the Convention vote actually required a voluntary postal ballot. After all, this was merely a one-off vote for half the delegates to a convention which might one day lead to further constitutional votes – rather than a standard general election to decide the government of the day. The Government argued that delivering ballot papers to voters' homes (where they could properly be mulled over and returned or destroyed depending on voters' preference) was actually a fairer way to read the public mind. For some months, it seemed, neither side thought the Convention was sufficiently important to be worth a compromise.

The initial rejection of the Convention Bill suggested that the Senate majority cared more about compulsory voting than an 'Australian head of state'. It seemed as though a republic was too important to be worth a backward step (by accepting a once-only voluntary vote) – or insufficiently important to be worth a forward step (by spending an extra $15 million on the standard

election procedure). Constitutional passions, it seemed, ran either too strongly or too weakly to produce an outcome. So, having first lobbied senators to reject the Government's legislation for what he had described as a 'wasteful talking shop' [*Australian,* 1 June, 1996], Malcolm Turnbull did a complete about face and, eventually, door-knocked them imploring support for the Government's Bill.

During the Convention debate, the Prime Minister had announced that the Federal Parliamentary Liberal Party's Convention delegates would be himself, Treasurer Peter Costello, Attorney-General Daryl Williams, Senate Leader Robert Hill, and Senator Jocelyn Newman, the senior woman Cabinet Minister – plus four delegates whose names would be drawn from a hat.

The draw produced four men, all supporters of the constitutional status quo, three of whom were from South Australia. Inside the Liberal party room, republicans, feminists and the advocates of balance among the States demanded a different result. One of the South Australian male MPs offered to withdraw – to be replaced, as it turned out, by a female republican (who also happened to be a South Australian).

When the Government announced the appointed delegates (and it turned out that only one of the eight under 25s was a declared republican) there was further unrest. One of the anti-republican nominees was a Queensland Young Liberal who had earlier been carpeted for 'rorting memberships' – but the more interesting point was how this was 'brought to the *Herald's* attention by moderate Liberals' angered by the Convention's composition [*Sydney Morning Herald,* 3 September, 1997].

The environmentally sustainable republic

The Senate's initial rejection of the Convention Bill posed problems for the Government too. The republican issue had engaged too many participants in public life simply to fade away. Whichever way it concluded, the debate required a climax which only government could provide. Scrapping the Convention would have meant finding another way to resolve the constitutional debate – or alienating the republican lobby inside the Liberal Party. When it went before the Senate for the third time in the last week of August, the Convention that no-one really wanted had become the escape hatch that everyone needed. So, when Tasmanian Green Senator Bob Brown announced that he was changing his vote 'to bring about a fair, just, and environmentally sustainable republic' [*Australian Financial Review*, 1 September, 1997], metaphorically at least, all sides breathed a sigh of relief. The Australian public, as it happened, seemed little moved either way, with 58% telling Newspoll that the threatened cancellation of the Convention would make no difference [*Australian,* 2 July, 1997].

The new timetable is for a postal ballot for Convention delegates to begin in November and close on December 9 with the Convention itself taking place in February 1998. The Convention will focus on three basic questions: should Australia become a republic; what sort of republic might Australia become; and what arrangements, if any, might be put in place to facilitate such a change.

Republicans will highlight the 'threshold question' – the self-evident absurdity (as they see it) of having a 'foreign head of state'. Once that essential point is grasped, they think, the details of an Australian republic are a second order issue. Anti-republicans, on the other hand, will demand to know the terms and conditions of an Australian republic. They will argue that considering the republican principle – without knowing the republican practice – resembles asking people to buy without seeing the merchandise.

There is no doubt that the 'foreign head of state' annoys many Australians enough to justify a constitutional blind date. But quite a few instinctive republicans can be counted upon to hesitate in the face of this 'blank cheque' approach to constitutional reform. As prominent Victorian Liberal MP Petro Georgiou has said, it is:

> ... not far-fetched to foresee a president acting against a scandal ridden government that was endangering crucial national interests. Nor are presidential interventions in the case of impasse between the House of Representatives and the Senate beyond anticipation. One thing is certain – there would be frictions, uncertainties and new accommodations that over time would profoundly change our system of government.

Speech to Young Liberals, 11 August, 1996

Try as the republican movement will, it may be all-but-impossible to consider the 'foreign Queen' issue and the 'what sort of republic' question in isolation – because attitudes to one largely determine a response to the other.

As Churchill might have said, this is not the end (of the constitutional issue) nor even the beginning of the end. But it is the end of the beginning. Five years after Paul Keating 'came out' as a republican prime minister, a definitive process is finally under way. The long phoney war is over. The fate of the Australian Constitution is coming out of the hands of boosters, pollsters and pundits and into the hands of the people.

CHAPTER FIVE

The 'foreign queen'

'**D**O YOU – or don't you – want an Australian head of state?'.
That was the simple question Paul Keating posed in his
effort to win the republican argument. It was as stark as 'do you
– or don't you – want a 15% tax on everything you buy?', the line
he had used to win the 1993 election.

At the heart of the republican position is the claim that no-
one can support a continuing role for the Crown in the Constitution
and still be a 'fair dinkum' Australian. As Keating once said:

> The republic… will be important to everyone who believes in a bigger,
> larger Australia, one where people do have a belief in ourselves and in
> the country.

At the first big republican gathering after the 1996 election,
former Keating speechwriter Michael Fullilove reworked the
Keating proposition into the demand that Australia have 'a
resident for president'.

The republicans hope that this 'resident for president'
refrain will be to Australia's constitutional debate what 'liberty,
equality, fraternity' was to the French Revolution. But the 'foreign
head of state' argument raises two questions: is it true; and does
it matter?

The Australian Constitution does not provide for a head of

state. The Constitution provides for a Queen, a Governor-General and an Executive Council – but the term 'head of state' is entirely absent from the Australian Constitution as, indeed, it is absent from most others.

The 'head of state' concept seems to have originated in diplomacy rather than law, to distinguish those who are entitled to 21 gun salutes from those who are not, rather than to identify who really runs a country. The question of who is a country's head of state depends on whether the term refers to status or function. If the head of state is the person at the top of the protocol pecking order, the Queen is indeed Australia's head of state. But if the head of state is someone exercising power (real or ceremonial) over the nation, the Governor-General is the better qualified candidate.

Around the world, heads of state typically command the armed forces, summon and prorogue legislatures, appoint ministers to serve at their pleasure and sign bills into law. Some heads of state (such as the King of Spain and the President of Ireland) exercise their powers in a largely ceremonial capacity. Others (such as the US President and the Sultan of Brunei) run the executive government. Some, in other words, are team captains. Others are game umpires.

The preamble to the Australian Constitution states the desire of the then colonies to unite in 'one indissoluble Federal Commonwealth under the Crown'. Thereafter, it carefully distinguishes between the two elements of the Crown – 'the Queen' and the 'Governor-General' – one a monarch and the other, although technically a viceroy, the wielder of all the Crown's powers in Australia. Although section 61 vests the executive power of the Commonwealth in the Queen, this power is 'exercisable by the Governor-General as the Queen's representative'. Section 64 gives the Governor-General power to appoint ministers. Section 68 makes the Governor-General commander-in-chief. Section 5 says that the Governor-General is to summon and dissolve Parliament. Section 58 provides for the Governor-General to assent to laws.

As has already been noted, in 1975 when the Speaker of the House of Representatives sought the Queen's intervention to overturn the Governor-General's dismissal of the Prime Minister, the Queen's Secretary observed that:

> The Queen has no part in the decisions which the Governor-General must take in accordance with the Constitution...

and

> ... It would not be proper for (her) to intervene in matters which are so clearly placed within the jurisdiction of the Governor-General by the Constitution.

Even the Republic Advisory Committee concluded that the Queen's *sole remaining power* under the Australian Constitution was to appoint a Governor-General – and that this could only be exercised on the advice of the Australian Prime Minister.

On the basis that he looks like a head of state, sounds like a head of state and acts like a head of state, the Governor-General is Australia's head of state. Bill Hayden called himself head of state when he was Governor-General. The 1995 edition of the Australian Government Directory says that the Governor-General 'is the head of state in whom the executive power of the Commonwealth is vested'. At least one Australian Act of Parliament – the Crimes (Internationally Protected Persons) Act 1976 – provides that, in relation to Australia, the head of state is the Governor-General. And in his Parliamentary Statement calling for a republic, Keating himself described the Governor-General as head of state.

As at mid 1997, Governors-General have made 51 state and official visits to 33 countries since Sir Paul Hasluck made the first official overseas visit by a Governor-General in 1971. Sir Ninian Stephen once cancelled a foreign trip because he was not going to receive head of state treatment – but went after the Indonesians had resolved the protocol issue.

The fact that some foreigners (including some who should know better such as, on at least one occasion, the US State Department) are ignorant of the Governor-General's status is their problem rather than ours. In a report to the Government after a trade-boosting mission, Governor-General Hayden complained that the new Government of Kazakhstan had not fully grasped his role and status. This is no more surprising than the difficulties other countries might have had with the role of Deng Xiaoping in China or the relationship between the Party and the Government in the former Soviet Union.

Although the Constitution states that the Governor-General represents the Queen (and, in that sense, can be said to be subordinate to her), it also states that he exercises all the Queen's powers under the Constitution (and does so, as we have seen, in his own right). Although, as a courtesy, governors-general have always reported regularly to the Queen, they do not answer to her. The Queen's 'primacy of honour' does not necessarily mean, as republicans insist, that the Queen must be Australia's head of state – since all her powers are exercised by someone else and, in any event, are derived from the Australian people under the Australian Constitution. She is the Queen, no more and no less.

Because the Crown is the legal cornerstone of the Australian Constitution, many academics (including, most recently, the British political scientist Vernon Bogdanor) have concluded that the Queen is Australia's head of state. However, the longest-serving Secretary to the Governor-General, Sir David Smith, has said that although the Queen is the symbol of our constitutional arrangements, the Governor-General is our effective head of state exercising all the Queen's powers under the Constitution, even when the Queen is present in Australia.

In 1901, Quick and Garran quoted a former Governor-General of Canada's description of himself as 'the head of a constitutional state'. Melbourne University's Professor Brian Galligan has described the Governor-General as head of state. Professor Colin Howard has said that 'certain matters of ceremony and courtesy apart, the head of state in Australia is not the Queen but the Governor-General'. Sydney University's Professor Patrick Lane has declared that:

> The Australianisation of the Crown is now complete. The Governor-General... has become, in substance, an Australian institution... This Australian monarch is less like a monarch than a president while still standing aloof from politics.

Australian, **29 September, 1994**

In his Commentary on the Constitution, Lane declares that the High Court, if called upon, would find that the Governor-General is, in fact, our functional head of state.

Mean-minded chauvinism

Australians have no problem with foreigners running our largest corporation or our biggest police force but it is almost inconceivable that a non-Australian could be appointed Governor-General – which testifies to a recognition that he is our ultimate civic leader. In any event, when the ARM was criticised for giving the expatriate writer Robert Hughes top-billing at a rally, Turnbull responded:

> What sort of mean-minded chauvinism is that?... I mean, surely as an intellectual he's entitled to be judged on the merit or demerit of his ideas not where he lives.

AM, **3 December, 1996**

If, in fact, the Governor-General is Australia's head of state, republicanism seems less like nationalism and more like chauvinism: a bad case of 'let's piss off the poms'. The 'do you – or don't you – want an Australian head of state?' question is tough on Governor-General Sir William Deane who is an Australian citizen in good standing (as all his predecessors have been since 1965).

A standard republican complaint is the Queen's bit-part in promoting British exports. A particular grievance is the Queen's supposed support for European farm policies which hurt Australian exports. Some grizzle about her (presumed) barracking for England against Australia at cricket (even though quite a few perfectly good Australians feel the pangs of shared loyalties when Australia plays their former home). If State Premiers can be good Australians even when they are fiercely attacking the policies of the Australian Government, if migrants can invest much of their time and emotion in their former countries without being any less Australian and if run-of-the-mill citizens can wear several hats on any one day (company representative, family member, religious adherent, sporting partisan), the Queen is capable of exercising more than one role at one time.

No doubt the Crown's role does sometimes raise questions of conflict of interest – such as when the Royal Yacht was requested for the Manchester Olympic bid and the Queen declined on the grounds that two of her cities were in contention. There is no reason to think that these need become unmanageable. It would be difficult for one person to be at war with herself so in the event of the Queen of Australia's army finding itself at war with the Queen of the United Kingdom's army, new constitutional arrangements would almost certainly be required (and new armies too!). But short of fundamental conflict between Australia and Britain, sharing a titular head presents no insoluble problems in theory and has never presented any in practice.

Australia is as independent as we could possibly be. Elizabeth II is Queen of Australia not by virtue of British law but by virtue of Australian law. As the British monarch she is just another head of state and even in her Australian capacity she is a titular head of state whose Australian powers are exercised by a distinguished Australian. The British Government is just another friendly foreign Government. Australia maintains its own armed forces and its own diplomatic corps. We sign our own treaties and award our own decorations. We pass our own laws and make our own decisions.

Like all nations we sometimes defer to outside interests. We choose not to defy the United Nations and we have little option but to accommodate international market forces. We seek American military support and we have been known to soft-pedal human rights abuses in Indonesia. But realpolitik – not lack of independence – explains any deference. Australia has an affinity with many nations but none is our master. We are a separate people with a separate destiny and – as far as is possible in the real world – we do exactly what we choose.

'Mainstream' republicans – or at least those running the Australian Republican Movement – say that they do not want to change our system of Government, just the identity of our head of state. They say that we should be an independent nation with our own distinct identity and a distinguished Australian as head of state. That, in fact, is what we are. We have an Australian as our constitutional head of state. It is the Governor-General, and not the Queen, who exercises the powers of the head of state, so that becoming a republic, even on the most benign interpretation, means a substantial constitutional re-write – just to confirm what Australia already has.

If the advocates of constitutional change were talking about overlap and duplication between the different tiers of Government, creeping centralism via the Federal Government's financial power, or misuse of the foreign affairs power, they would at least be addressing practical problems. Instead, they focus on a republic which even they say is a purely symbolic issue. This is the inherent implausibility at the heart of the republican idea. If the republicans are right and nothing will really change, why bother? If, on the other hand, they're playing down the extent of flow-on changes, why take the risk?

President versus Governor-General

The real choice is not between the Queen and an Australian as head of state but between a familiar Australian institution, the Governor-General, and a presidency which would break new ground. Judged against the only criterion that mattered – how will it improve Australia's system of government? – becoming a republic risks a great deal of uncertainty and division to fix what is, at worst, the minor problem of the address of our titular head of state.

To the extent that it was thought about at the time, we entrenched the monarchy in our Constitution and, more recently, kept it in the Australia Act because it was in Australia's best interests to do so. We have kept it because it has served Australia's own purposes. And we will retain it only as long as there is something in it for us. We have been fully independent for at least 50 years and the Crown has never stopped us from putting Australia first.

CHAPTER SIX

What sort of republic?

REPUBLICS come in all sorts of constitutional shapes and ethical sizes ranging from the United States to Rwanda. It is, of course, not entirely fair to equate an Australian republic with Russia, Libya, Iran, the Congo – or whichever other republic is the world's latest disaster area – because any Australian republic would inherit much of the stability of Australian society and would retain for the time being its existing constitutional culture. However, it is not only legitimate but necessary to ask 'what sort of republic?' *before* deciding whether a republic makes sense. An 'in-principle' position cannot be sustained because becoming a republic means moving from what we have to a specific republican alternative.

Like republics, Australian republicans are a mixed bag. Some have a much wider constitutional agenda than simply changing the arrangements concerning the head of state. For instance, former Queensland Premier Wayne Goss has called for the abolition of the Senate to be considered as part of the republican process [*Australian,* 13 May, 1993]. Prominent ALP left-winger, Lindsay Tanner, has sought to 'pursue broader constitutional issues within the republican framework' such as the abolition of the States and a bill of rights [*Canberra Times,* 6 July, 1993]. Former NSW Liberal

Minister Bruce Baird has called for a republic trifecta, a new flag, new anthem and new constitution in time for the Olympics [*Sydney Morning Herald*, 14 August, 1996]. The Australian Republican Party chief, Peter Considine, wants a major constitutional re-write to accompany an elected presidency.

There is, however, a republican 'establishment' – centred on the Australian Republican Movement – with the oft-stated objective to change the head of state but not the system of government. To achieve this, however, republicans must solve the basic problem of ensuring that a president will act in more-or-less the same way as a governor-general.

Even within the ARM, there are quite divergent views on how this might be done. Most leading ARM members support a president elected by parliament – not because they are opposed to popular election, but because they believe popular election would mean, in effect, a partisan political contest for the one office which is currently above and beyond party politics.

ARM luminaries usually want a president to exercise more-or-less the same powers as the Governor-General exercises now, but there are significant differences on how this might be achieved. Whether a president can achieve the Governor-General's insulation from the political process or exercise the same powers as a head of state governed by monarchical conventions is by no means clear despite the ARM's best efforts.

The Republic Advisory Committee (which included leading ARM figures such as Turnbull as chairman, and Winterton and Hirst as members) canvassed four options for the selection of a president: appointment by the Prime Minister; appointment by the Parliament (by simple or special majority); popular election; and appointment by an electoral college of distinguished Australians.

Prime ministerial appointment raises the possibility (at least in theory) of the head of state as prime ministerial poodle. Parliamentary appointment (especially by two-thirds majority) raises the possibility of a head of state with greater political authority than the Prime Minister. Popular election has the same drawback – with the added difficulty of political party involvement. An electoral college could avoid the 'head of state as lackey' or 'head of state as rival' problems – while (compared with direct popular election or even election by the Parliament) raising problems about the legitimacy of a president so chosen.

The Committee canvassed a similarly broad range of options to deal with the powers now exercised by the Governor-General (who, on a literal reading of the Australian Constitution, seems to be the most powerful figure in our political system). The fact that the Governor-General's only personal power is to act as constitutional umpire in rare moments of political crisis and otherwise to act on the advice of the Prime Minister and Cabinet does not diminish the importance of clarifying powers based on tradition and convention (especially when it is proposed to remove the source of those conventions).

Without further specification, there is little reason to think that conventions governing the relationship between monarch and executive government would also govern the relationship between president and executive government. Prior to the Committee's report, leading republicans had generally claimed that becoming a republic involved little more than going through our existing Constitution and substituting 'President' for 'Queen' or 'Governor-General'. Indeed, virtually until the day he released the Committee's report, Turnbull had claimed that becoming a republic is 'quite a simple matter. All that is required is to delete references to the Queen and Governor-General and replace them with references to a president and then state how the president is to be appointed' [*The Age*, 2 August, 1993].

Tippex republicanism

However, doubts about how Westminster conventions could translate into a republican constitution led the Committee to concede that 'Tippex' republicanism (which said nothing about the extent of the head of state's powers) risked giving a president 'potentially autocratic powers' [Report, p. 116]. The report considered three options for presidential powers: partial codification; full codification; or leaving them as they are, subject to unwritten conventions.

The report argued that some aspects of the reserve powers – such as the Governor-General's ability to dismiss a prime minister trying to govern without supply – were far from clear. In fact, under the existing Constitution, the Governor-General's power to dismiss a prime minister who retains the confidence of a lower house majority is a matter for controversy rather than doubt.

Under the Constitution as it stands, the head of state acts on ministerial advice except in emergencies. In extremis, the Prime Minister and the Governor-General have the ability to sack one another – which is an important check on the actions of each. The Committee's report suggests a constitutional provision to the effect that a republican head of state should exercise his or her powers:

'In accordance with the constitutional conventions which related to the powers… of the Governor-General' *but that* 'nothing in this section shall have the effect of turning constitutional conventions into rules of law.

Report, p. 94

Given that the head of state's discretionary powers should not, the report says, be subject to review by the High Court, a president would be able exercise these powers very much as he or she sees fit. Under the Constitution as it stands, a governor-general with ideas above his station can be dismissed. But dismissing a president elected by a two-thirds majority of the Parliament would be no easy matter. The report concluded that substituting 'president' for 'Governor-General' in the existing Constitution and saying nothing about the conventions would give a president 'potentially autocratic powers' [Report, p. 116].

At present, the Governor-General can be sacked with a message to Buckingham Palace. This arrangement reflects the fact that the head of state theoretically represents someone else. Instant dismissal would be quite inappropriate for a president – yet is the key sanction against improper use of the head of states's extensive formal powers.

Under the Keating republican model, a president ruling by decree is not impossible. Without the potential for legal challenge, a provision applying the existing conventions to a president would be no more than a gentleman's agreement. Dismissal is the key restraint on presidential impropriety. Yet under the republicans' preferred model of a president elected (and dismissed) by a two thirds majority of both houses of parliament, a president with the support of just one third of MPs could virtually do what he liked (to say nothing of one who decided to prorogue parliament to prevent its meeting).

The report's authors suggest that the president should seek a High Court declaration if he or she thinks that the Government might be contravening a 'fundamental provision' of the Constitution. Although the report seems to contemplate judicial review of prime ministerial (rather than presidential) acts, it still has the potential to involve the High Court in the most highly charged political crises. As former Victorian Governor Richard McGarvie has said:

> The novelty of bringing the courts into the political process... would
> be as damaging to that process as to the courts.

In such an event, the fury that greeted Sir John Kerr would be visited on the High Court with serious implications for the court's standing.

Defusing future crises was not the only reason the Committee wanted to reduce constitutional uncertainty. 'It is in the public interest' said the report, 'that there be a higher level of awareness about the Constitution and this awareness would be enhanced if the Constitution provided a more accurate description of the way we are governed' [Report, p. 98]. The Committee seemed to take it for granted that the Constitution should serve as a political text book. But, as Lloyd Waddy has said, 'you don't learn much about how a marriage works by studying the certificate'. Malcolm Mackerras has observed that the need to serve as a Political Science I primer would produce a 'loose-leaf constitution' and that the country which most frequently up-dated its constitution and most strove to have it reflect current political thinking was, in fact, the former Soviet Union.

A loose-leaf constitution

Keating's parliamentary response to the Committee's report failed to resolve the detail of how a president might exercise his powers. The fact that Keating's republican blue-print did not actually contain a draft republican constitution hints at the extraordinary difficulty of giving a president the same role as a governor-general and effectively placing the restraints of a constitutional monarchy on a republican president.

Keating envisaged that all the powers which the Governor-General currently exercises on ministerial advice would – by express constitutional provision – be exercised by a president on ministerial advice. However, the powers which the Governor-

General currently exercises without advice – the 'reserve powers of the Crown' – would continue, under the Keating model, to be exercised according to the discretion of the president. There would be an express constitutional provision to the effect that the reserve powers would be exercised under the same conventions as applied to the Governor-General and that the exercise of these powers would not be reviewable by any court.

But, as the former High Court Chief Justice Sir Harry Gibbs has pointed out, it is easier to declare that the Court will not be involved than to ensure that it actually refrains from 'improving' things. Gibbs said that the attempt to keep the High Court from adjudicating on any exercise of the reserve powers may not work, given the Court's 'ingenuity' in discovering ways to be involved [*Australian*, 21 June, 1995].

It will be much easier to keep the High Court out of politics than it will be to keep politics out of the operation of a future presidency – despite 'establishment' republicans' insistence that the requirement of a two thirds majority of both houses of parliament for presidential election will ensure that a president has bi-partisan support.

Since the current Senate voting procedure was adopted in 1949, no Government has had a two thirds majority in its own right (although the Fraser Government in 1975 needed only the support of Liberal maverick Steele Hall or conservative independent Brian Harradine to attain such a majority). However, the winner-takes-all Senate voting system which applied before 1949 made two thirds majorities quite common. Five of the 18 elections prior to 1949 produced governments with two thirds majorities in both houses of parliament.

The Commonwealth Electoral Act (which determines voting systems) can be changed by a simple majority in both Houses.

While prime minister, Keating indicated that changing the Senate voting system was a 'major and legitimate issue' and made no promise to entrench the current voting system in a republican constitution [*Australian,* 19 May, 1994]. Subsequently, various Liberal luminaries have speculated about changing the Senate voting system to entrench big party control – so without constitutional entrenchment, the Senate voting system will remain a weak link in any republican scheme to ensure that a president has bi-partisan support.

In the wake of the Republic Advisory Committee Report, three key members published their own republican blueprints in an effort to solve the republican dilemma – in particular, the key problem of whether the head of state should be empowered to dismiss a prime minister who is acting unconstitutionally.

The events of 1975 mean that advocates of a republic cannot gloss over the reserve powers. They need to convince the 'Labor' viewpoint that 1975 is highly unlikely to recur – and to convince the 'Liberal' viewpoint that there will be no diminution of the reserve powers. Convinced monarchists will reject a republic regardless of the constitutional details. But republicans could reject any particular republican proposal unless it gets this point right.

Malcolm Turnbull's draft republican constitution follows the suggestions made in the Committee report. If the House of Representatives has passed a motion of no confidence in the Prime Minister and does not pass a confidence motion within three days, the President can dismiss the Prime Minister. And if the President believes that the Government is contravening a 'fundamental provision' of the Constitution or is 'not complying with the order of a court', the President can seek an explanation from the Prime Minister and then seek relief from the High Court.

If the Court finds that the Constitution is being breached or the law flouted, the President may dissolve the House of Representatives and may also dismiss the Prime Minister and appoint someone else to maintain the administration of the Commonwealth pending an election [Turnbull, p. 275].

If the circumstances of 1975 were repeated, the President would be required to approach the Court seeking a judgment about the constitutionality of governing without supply and the legality of writing IOUs to the banks, prior to dissolving the Parliament and dismissing the Prime Minister. Compared with what actually took place in 1975, at the very least, this would prolong the crisis and expose the High Court to the same partisan rancour which engulfed Kerr.

Many republicans feel very strongly about codification of the reserve powers. Turnbull has dismissed as 'ludicrous' Gareth Evans' suggestion that there would never be agreement on codifying the powers and that, therefore, it should not even be tried. Turnbull said:

> Almost every country in the world defines, in its constitution, the scope of the powers of the head of government and the head of state. Why are Australians so peculiarly intellectually deficient as not to be able to do it?
>
> *Sydney Morning Herald,* **18 May, 1995**

By contrast, Professor George Winterton's draft republican constitution merely provides that the powers of the President shall be those of the Governor-General at the time immediately before the transition to a republic, until such time as a two thirds majority of both Houses of Parliament decides otherwise [Winterton, p. 20]. There are three problems with Winterton's approach: First, it does not solve the objection to the head of state's ability to sack a prime minister; second, it does not protect the principle of the head of state's ability to dismiss a prime minister; and third, it gives to the Parliament – and denies to the people – explicit constitution-making power. In short, Winterton's compromise has something in it to offend just about everyone.

John Hirst, the third senior member of the Republican Movement to draft a constitution, provides in his version that the President may dissolve the House of Representatives and dismiss the Prime Minister if the Government 'is breaching the Constitution or persisting in other unlawful behaviour' and that the exercise of this power is not reviewable by any court [Hirst, p. 130]. Hirst's constitution has the advantage of neither embroiling the High Court in the decisions of the head of state nor giving Parliament backdoor power over the Constitution – at the price of confirming (and strengthening) the head of state's power to dismiss an elected government.

Turnbull, Winterton and Hirst are distinguished intellectuals without any hands-on experience of government. Highly committed republicans aside, those who have seen the system from the inside (such as former Governor-General Hayden) are generally sceptical about schemes to change the power or tenure of the head of state – without also creating flow-on changes to Australia's system of government. Republicans have tried to dismiss Hayden as a republican turn-coat who has 'taken the king's shilling'. Hayden's fears, however, have recently been amplified by Richard McGarvie, the Labor-leaning lawyer and judge whom John Cain appointed Governor of Victoria.

Democracy in peril

Shortly after leaving Government House, McGarvie detailed his concerns in a widely reported paper (released on 30 April, 1997) titled 'Our Democracy in Peril'. McGarvie refused to take sides on the 'monarchy versus republic' question but stated his conviction that both a popularly elected president or a president elected (and dismissed) by a two thirds majority of both Houses of Parliament threatened Australia's established democratic system of government. Although McGarvie's warning was dismissed by Turnbull as 'hysterical and alarmist' [*Australian,* 2 May, 1997], leading republicans have been slow to refute his contention that a virtually unsackable president poses serious problems for the stability of our system of government.

McGarvie's paper is probably the single most important contribution to debate over the mechanics of constitutional change because it is based not on emotional commitment to one side or another but on practical experience of the checks and balances built into the existing system of government. McGarvie stresses the importance of the unwritten constitutional conventions governing the conduct of the Crown. These cannot be enforced in any court and derive their power entirely from the Prime Minister's ability to dismiss the Governor-General (or, in the United Kingdom, Parliament's ability to depose the monarch).

McGarvie says:

> It is crucial to our democracy, that the Governor-General always be liable to prompt dismissal for breach of convention.
>
> **McGarvie, p. 6**

He states that:

> Both models for an elected republican president (popular election or parliamentary election) would ruin our democracy by first destroying the basic constitutional convention (that the Crown only acts on ministerial advice). It would cease to be binding because it would have lost its effective sanction of dismissal. Democracy would unravel. We would be forgetting the lessons of history that you don't put people in positions of great power unless they are subject to democratic control. When the basic constitutional convention withers so does the democratic control.
>
> **McGarvie, p. 8**

Once in office, says McGarvie, a president requiring a two-thirds majority of both houses of parliament to be dismissed would be virtually unsackable.

> The theory that the Opposition would join the Government for a two thirds majority to remove a republican president who was frustrating the Government by defying convention cannot stand up to scrutiny in clear Australian daylight. Say you had a president who, at a time when the Government's popularity with the electorate had slumped, rejected Ministers' advice to assent to an unpopular government bill which had passed both houses. Usually the Opposition, of whichever side of politics, would be more likely to commend the president for recognising what a bad government it was than to join in a resolution of dismissal.
>
> **McGarvie, p. 9**

In any event, says McGarvie, 'a president with an instinct for self-defence could avoid a resolution of dismissal by exercising the power to prorogue (adjourn) parliament or to dissolve it' (p. 9). McGarvie's strictures would also apply to a president appointed or dismissed by a simple parliamentary majority. Although such a president would have less authority to flout constitutional conventions (and less stature as anything other than a tool of the Government of the day), he could equally contrive to frustrate his own dismissal by the device of avoiding a parliamentary sitting. Hence, any republic in which a president is not subject to instant dismissal – and in which he retains significant 'reserve' powers – runs the risk that, in times of crisis, the president will make his own rules.

It is all-but-inevitable that election of any sort will involve politics because 'getting the numbers' – even amongst a select group – nearly always involves trading favours. In the United States, Senate approval of Supreme Court judges has become a pitched battle with the candidate's past raked over for ideological error and with ultimate choices made along party lines. In Ireland, the (largely ceremonial) presidency is a fiercely-fought-over political football. The most recent president is widely regarded as a breath of fresh air – but the contest which gave victory to Mary Robinson was the Hibernian equivalent of Janine Haines beating Paul Keating.

Getting the numbers

In Australia, MPs' ballots for positions whose occupants are theoretically impartial (such as the speakership of the House or presidency of the Senate) are always decided on party lines and the occupants are expected to honour their political debts. In Australian practice, 'fairness' in these offices means restraining the worst excesses of partisan behaviour – not treating both sides impartially.

McGarvie makes the point that, regardless of whether presidents are elected by parliament or the people, the office and its occupant will be very different to that of Governor-General.

> If a president is elected by a two thirds majority of a joint sitting, it would be naive to assume there would not be parliamentary enquiries into suitability – as occurs with Supreme Court judges in the United States. Baseless but wounding allegations of disgraceful conduct would be prone to be made there or via internet or overseas television where there is now little protection. Why should people of repute like those the community has expected to be Governors-General in the past enter that bear pit? Presidents would be very different people from what Governors-General have been.
>
> Unless a multi-millionaire, a person could only campaign in the electorate for the position of president if supported by a political party. To secure election, policies would be stated and expected to be pursued upon election. The president would inevitably be a party politician with popular election winning skills – a person vastly different from what Australians expect in a Governor-General.
>
> **McGarvie, p. 12**

Australians' poll-confirmed desire to popularly elect a president suggests their belief that the people are better judges of a president's suitability than the politicians. 'Would you trust the same people who elected Mal Colston and Noel Crichton-Browne as Deputy Presidents of the Senate', the thinking seems to run, 'to elect a president of Australia?'. The fact that most republican proposals for electing a president involve fancy franchises is an acknowledgment of the general public's apparent desire to avoid a politician in the top job.

Republicans' reliance on a two thirds majority of both Houses of Parliament to guarantee an outstanding presidential choice often seems like the triumph of hope over experience. Someone to whom neither side objects is more likely to be a political nobody than a great leader – a sportsman or an artist who can be counted upon to lack the guile or inclination to stand up to the politicians, someone who is beneath the fray rather than above it. And this is the best outcome that can reasonably be expected from a collegial election.

Almost certainly, none of the most recent governors-general would have served as head of state in an Australian republic: Sir Zelman Cowen (as a distinguished legal academic), Sir Ninian Stephen and Sir William Deane (as former High Court judges) would have been unlikely to submit to the indignity of parliamentary examination; and Bill Hayden, like Sir Paul Hasluck before him, was far too effective a politician to command bi-partisan support prior to his appointment.

John Hirst has tried to circumvent this problem by proposing a two stage process: First, the Chief Justices of the High Court and the State Supreme Courts, the Speakers of the various Australian Parliaments, plus senior members chosen by lot from the Order of Australia would meet in secret to choose three candidates. Second, the Parliament would elect one of the three by a two thirds majority. Hirst's views are worthy of respect. Yet it is an extraordinary amount of secrecy for a democratic system and a huge amount of trouble for a position which is supposed to have largely ceremonial functions.

The fate of the speakership in a highly politicised system dominated by prime ministers who often regard politics as total war, suggests that McGarvie is right to worry that presidents elected by the Parliament might turn out to be quite different from governors-general representing the Queen.

Bill Hayden's pre-retirement comments about euthanasia and gay 'marriage' and Sir William Deane's frequently articulated social conscience are a reminder of the head of state's capacity to give a lead to the nation. These comments also illustrate the fine line between challenging individuals' consciences and challenging political parties' policies. A president could be expected to offer more, rather than less, of this type of leadership – and to show less, rather than more, of the Governor-General's traditional discretion. With a two thirds majority of both Houses of Parliament required for dismissal as well as appointment, a recalcitrant president would have a great deal of political authority as well as constitutional power.

Overseas experience largely bears out McGarvie's warnings about the politicisation of a presidency. The difference between the Australian Governor-General and the presidents of the world's republics is not that the Governor-General is never a former politician – but that presidents are nearly always current politicians. Whatever the Governor-General did before assuming office, once appointed, he or she is expected to act with complete indifference to party political outcomes. However 'ceremonial' presidents might be, they are always the product of a political system and are usually expected to support the political bloc which put them into office.

As long as the head of state is immersed in the traditions which have governed the Crown, a republic might make very little difference. Some Australians would miss a much admired monarch, links with an ancient constitutional order, involvement with an international institution shared with other countries – but most, perhaps, would be oblivious to the change.

A Weimar-style republic?

The risk would come with the appointment of a celebrity whose self-esteem exceeded his judgment or a mediocrity easily out-stared by the occupant of the Lodge. Under such circumstances, the 'establishment' republic could degenerate into fighting between Yarralumla and the Lodge, as president and prime minister struggle for the upper hand in an untried system. The risk is a Weimar-style republic with the prospect of chaos or autocracy as the system tries to sustain one government with two bosses.

Serious republicans know that the attempt to corral the President by stating that his or her powers will be those of the Governor-General will not work. This is why Donald Horne declared, on the eve of the Keating announcement that, without a clear statement of the President's powers, 'even I will vote 'no' to a referendum' [*Sydney Morning Herald*, 3 June, 1995].

CHAPTER SEVEN

The McGarvie 'republic'

R ICHARD McGARVIE has not just mounted the most sustained critique of the 'Keating republic' but has also made the most sophisticated attempt to resolve the difficulties of becoming a republic.

The Governor-General does not actually wield the powers notionally given under the Constitution because (quite apart from inhibitions based on constitutional practice) the Prime Minister would instantly dismiss any governor-general who tried to exercise them. McGarvie identifies preserving the Prime Minister's ability to dismiss the head of state as the key to a safe republic. After retiring as Governor, McGarvie outlined the changes necessary, in his view, to achieve an Australian republic within the existing constitutional structure:

> The organisational change is to set up a Constitutional Council of three eminent Australians to take the place of the Queen in performing the one power she now performs – appointing or dismissing a governor-general as advised by the Prime Minister. The Council would be created under the Australian Constitution, which would by formula auto-matically select its membership from persons retired from non-political, constitutional positions of trust such as governors-general, governors and High Court judges. It would only have that one power of the Queen and would perform it in the same way on the Prime Minister's advice.
>
> **McGarvie, p. 4**

McGarvie proposes an 'order of succession' to the Constitutional Council among retired governors-general, governors, and Federal judges plus a weighting formula to ensure at least one woman member. The nature of the Council's membership, he thinks, makes it a suitable substitute for the Queen in ratifying the Prime Minister's choice as head of state.

McGarvie stresses that this is the key change required to move to the republican equivalent of our present system. In an article published while he was serving Governor of Victoria, he said:

> Should the power to appoint or dismiss the Governor on the Premier's advice be transferred to a Constitutional Council created under the Victorian Constitution and the Governor become the constitutional head of the State of Victoria instead of being the representative of that head, and the Queen's right to exercise powers when actually in Victoria be ended, then Victoria would have a republican form of government.
>
> *The Parliamentarian,* **July 1994**

Organisationally, he may have a point as far as Victoria is concerned (although, even under the existing system, Australia is already a 'crowned republic'). *Constitutionally*, however, at least as far as the Commonwealth is concerned, more would be required. For Australia to become a republic, it would be necessary not only to find a suitable mechanism for appointing the head of state but also to write the Crown out of some 70 clauses in the existing Constitution and, in doing so, to say something about the reserve powers.

McGarvie thinks that the power of prime ministerial dismissal will ensure that governors-general (or presidents) do not expand their powers even in the absence of the conventions governing the Crown. Still, writing the Crown out of the Constitution without changing the scope of the Governor-General's legal power may be all-but-impossible even as a matter of legal drafting, as the difficulties republicans have had in detailing a new constitution seem to show.

As Sir Harry Gibbs has commented:

McGarvie does not deal with the question how the conventions which are observed by the Governor-General and Governors as representatives of a constitutional monarch would bind a president... [He] seems to assume that a president would regard them as applicable under a republic. This is a very large assumption and if wrong the position of the president would be immensely strengthened.

McGarvie thinks that 'solving' the problem of a president's appointment and dismissal also solves the problem of a president's powers. However, it is far from clear that his proposed Constitutional Council would be effective even as a legal or political substitute for the Queen, let alone as an adequate substitute for codification of any president's powers.

As Lloyd Waddy has pointed out, the Council:

Has no separate existence (unlike the Queen) and will be at best a shadowy presence of fluctuating members of the power elites, of former appointees of politicians, comprised probably of former or failed politicians.

The fact that members will include former governors-general or governors may not give the Council the standing McGarvie envisages for it because, under a republic, these positions are likely to become steadily politicised. Waddy says:

Even a Council comprised of McKell, Hasluck and Hayden, would command no bi-partisan or public acceptance at all – particularly when they explained that they had appointed (or dismissed) the head of state because the Prime Minister had told them to.

The biggest obstacle to McGarvie's 'republic', of course, is political. As Waddy says:

The people will never wear a head of state with huge powers appointed (even needing the added consent of a Constitutional Council) by the Prime Minister and liable to be sacked by the Prime Minister the moment he moves to defend the Constitution. The people wear it at present because they have a sense that the Queen cannot be manipulated and because no-one is quite sure how quickly or how publicly the Queen will act. A week, or even a day, is a long time in politics.

No doubt McGarvie thinks that the ex-vice-regal composition of the Council would ensure that the existing constitutional culture was maintained. Perhaps this constitutional equivalent of the apostolic succession would work; perhaps not, in which case, Australia would have substituted a system of cronyism for a tried and true method of ensuring a non-political head of state.

Even if McGarvie had produced an acceptable substitute for the Queen in her current role of appointing the effective head of state on prime ministerial advice, he would only have solved half the problem. To say that 'the head of state's powers don't matter a great deal because the Prime Minister can sack him if he gets out of line' is to give far too many hostages to fortune.

A monarchy without a monarch

At most, McGarvie has removed the Queen but not the Crown; or produced, if this be possible, a monarchy without the monarch because, in the absence of a safe alternative, it would be necessary to keep the Crown to guarantee the continuance of the conventions governing the exercise of the head of state's powers. McGarvie has not produced a republic, so much as a mechanism for a constitution without the Queen.

McGarvie has not published a draft constitutional amendment to give effect to a Constitutional Council. Appendix One of this book is an attempt to put his ideas into possible provisions of the Constitution. For simplicity, it provides that the Council shall comprise the three most recently retired State Governors.

The draft bill amends section 2 of the Constitution to declare that the Governor-General is the representative of the Crown and the Australian head of state. It also provides for the appointment (and dismissal) of the Governor-General by a Constitutional Council comprising the three most recently retired State governors acting on the advice of the Prime Minister. It further provides that the Governor-General (and members of the Constitutional Council) must be Australian citizens.

If, as McGarvie suggests, the Queen is to lose her chief constitutional role to appoint the Governor-General on prime ministerial advice, the rest of the Constitution (presumably) should reflect this change. Hence, the draft bill also includes a range of consequential or housekeeping changes. Together, they add up to a symbolically important shift of emphasis from a Queen of Australia to an Australian Crown and from a hereditary monarch (who is represented by a local viceroy) to an Australian head of state who embodies the Australian Crown.

In approximate order of symbolic significance, a 'McGarvie constitution' might alter Section 1 of the Constitution to vest the legislative power of the Commonwealth in the Governor-General (rather than the Queen), a Senate and a House of Representatives. It might amend Section 61 to vest the executive power of the Commonwealth in the Crown rather than the Queen herself; amend Section 34 to provide for MPs who are Australian citizens rather than subjects of the Queen; delete the provisions of Sections 58 and 60 allowing bills to be reserved 'for the Queen's pleasure'; and delete altogether Section 59 (providing for the Queen to disallow Australian Acts of Parliament).

All up, removing redundant or unnecessary references to the Queen in a 'McGarvie constitution' could involve 20 separate constitutional amendments. In addition, for consistency, the oath of office would need to be changed into a pledge to uphold the Australian Constitution.

Removing the 'foreign' Queen would also require amendments to the preamble to the Constitution: for instance, the substitution of 'Her Majesty's heirs and successors in the sovereignty of Australia' (instead of the United Kingdom). This would most likely require – in addition to a referendum to change the Constitution itself – uniform legislation from all seven Australian parliaments under the Australia Act.

A 'McGarvie constitution' would put beyond doubt the Governor-General's status as head of state (rather than mere viceroy). But the Crown would have to remain in the Constitution (to preserve the existing limitations on the head of state's powers) and the Queen would remain Queen of Australia by operation of the preamble to the Constitution.

The 1988 Constitutional Commission recommended the insertion of an additional power under section 51 enabling the Parliament to make laws for the 'succession to the throne and regency in the sovereignty of Australia'. Under the proposition sketched here, in an attempt to do justice to McGarvie's ideas, the Governor-General could be seen as a kind of permanent regent with the Constitutional Council as a kind of permanent council of regency to stand in for the Queen under an amended Constitution. The Queen would remain in the preamble to the Constitution as a kind of icon to enable the Governor-General to retain his existing role and functions.

McGarvie, in fact, describes his proposal for a Constitutional Council to appoint the head of state, not in terms of becoming a republic, but as 'patriating the remaining powers of head of state from the Queen to Australians' [McGarvie, p.7]. That, however, is one of the key problems with his proposal. As McGarvie himself acknowledges, if we are to become a republic, 95% of Australians want a president elected by the people or the parliament. Less than 5% want the Prime Minister to appoint a president. So even if his proposal were constitutionally safe, it would appeal more to lawyers than to voters.

In all likelihood, the McGarvie 'solution' would fail to please republicans while deeply alienating supporters of the constitutional status quo. There is, in any event, a much simpler (and safer) way to make concessions to republicanism without compromising the existing system of government (which I propose in the final chapter).

CHAPTER EIGHT

Republican arguments (and what's wrong with them)

REPUBLICANS typically claim that Australia must change its Constitution because:

a) we're no longer British and the Crown is offensive to migrants;

b) we'll never be truly independent and truly mature while the Queen of Australia is also Queen of the United Kingdom; and

c) becoming a republic is inevitable so Australians might as well do it now.

These arguments are advanced with deep conviction and emotional power but none has any particular logical force.

The idea that a multi-cultural Australia all-but-mandates a republic is, perhaps, one of the most pervasive features of the constitutional debate. How can migrants from Greece, Italy, Japan, Spain, Holland, Thailand and Tonga (all monarchies or ex-monarchies, incidentally) plus all the other nations whose people have emigrated to Australia accept as the Australian Queen someone who is also the British monarch? This is actually a rhetorical question rather than an argument and turns out to be a debating trick dressed up as logic. It boils down to the (false) syllogism: the monarchy comes from England; migrants don't come from England; therefore, migrants can't accept the monarchy.

To start with, there is no evidence that migrants are especially pro or anti-republican. The major pollsters do not normally identify respondents by ethnicity, presumably because of the difficulty of being precise about such a subjective concept and the intrinsic irrelevance of an Irish grandfather or Vietnamese mother to Australians' view of the Australian Constitution.

An AGB-McNair poll taken after the 1995 NSW State election showing that the Coalition had overwhelmingly won ethnic votes suggests that, if migrants support a republic, it does not necessarily change their votes [*Sydney Morning Herald*, 31 March, 1995]. There are prominent Australians of non-Anglo Celtic ethnic background on both sides of the debate and groups such as the NSW Ethnic Communities Council seem no less divided and uncertain about the question of becoming a republic than the wider Australian community.

'Ethnics' and 'Anglos'

In fact, despite Franca Arena's protestations, there is little poll evidence that 'ethnic' Australians differ from 'Anglo' Australians in their attitudes to the Crown. In an analysis of long-term poll trends, Macquarie University psephologist Murray Goot has observed that support for the monarchy remained relatively constant for most of the post-war period at the same time as Australia's ethnic make-up substantially changed. The conclusion he draws is that 'non-Anglo' migrants do not markedly differ from the rest of the population in their attitudes to the Crown [see Winterton, p. 78].

It seems odd that migrants would choose a new country while rejecting one of its significant national institutions. For all their understandable attachment to former homelands and familiar customs, migrants mostly desire to become Australian. Unlike the native born, migrants have made a conscious act of choice in favour of Australia. On this reckoning, the most that can be said of migrants is that – if they dislike the monarchy – their dislike cannot have been a very strong deterrent. They may have chosen Australia despite the Crown or in ignorance of the Crown. Still, they came here because they judged that Australia was a significantly more appealing place to live than their former homelands.

If there is some plausibility in the assumption that non-British migrants have little affection for the 'British' monarch, it also makes sense to say that their antipathy cannot have been very strong because, refugees aside, no-one made them choose Australia. It seems safe to assume that constitutional considerations were not uppermost in the minds of most migrants – yet the fact that they chose Australia suggests considerable warmth towards our way of life including (presumably) the stability and freedom built into our system of government.

If migrants to America can develop a cultural affinity for the Pilgrim Fathers, John Smith, George Washington and Abraham Lincoln, migrants to Australia can readily learn to appreciate the contribution of Aborigines, convicts and Anzacs. And if this is part of the cultural inheritance of all Australians, regardless of ethnic background, ethnicity should not preclude an affinity for the Crown under which Australia has become a free, fair and prosperous society.

Even if the Crown in Australia were nothing more than the 'British monarch', it would still be possible for migrants to appreciate and support an institution which had been part of Australia's constitutional furniture for 200 years. Yet the Australian Crown is quite different from the British Crown – principally because all the Crown's powers are exercised by a governor-general who is chosen for the job rather than born to it, is always a distinguished Australian citizen and acts (except in emergencies) on the advice of the Australian Prime Minister. The Australian Crown has become egalitarian and democratic in a way the British Crown never has – without trappings, titles and formality. The Australian Crown has taken on local characteristics just as Australian cricket soon lost 'gentlemen and players' snobbery.

Arguments based on ethnicity underestimate the extent of the 'inculturation' process and the speed with which migrants take on the attitudes of Australians (in addition to – and sometimes in contra-distinction to – the attitudes of their native land). Australia has been an immigrant society from its very beginnings and at least a quarter of the first white inhabitants – Irish convicts – can have had no great love for the Crown. Very soon, Australian-ness (in which the Crown was a benevolent force) began to displace Irish-ness (in which hostility to the Crown was almost second nature).

As a former leader of the Irish Republican Brotherhood, who became a member of the Queensland militia in 1888, explained:

> I was never a disloyalist. If we had the Government in Ireland we have here, I would have been wearing the Queen's uniform all my life.
>
> **Partington, p. 64**

Bishop James Quinn, who had no love for the English Benedictines originally presiding over the Australian Catholic Church, nevertheless declared that:

> Irish Catholics had fair play and fair recognition nowhere on Earth so unreservedly as in Australia.
>
> **Partington, p. 72**

Cardinal Patrick Moran was a mighty champion of the Irish-Catholic cause in Australia but regarded:

> Our colonial administration, linked as it is to the Crown of Great Britain, as the most perfect form of republican Government. It has all the freedom which a republican Government imparts, and it is free from

the many unpleasant influences to which, as in the United States, an elected head of a republic is subject.

Partington, p. 81

The most perfect form of republican government

The first organised contingent to serve in the Empire's wars was sent to the Sudan in 1885 by NSW Premier William Bede Dalley who remarked:

> All these years they have been calling us plotting Papists and Fenian rebels and the first men to serve the Queen are being sent by a Paddy and a Holy Roman.

Partington, p. 97

People who participate in the Australian way of life and who use the English language have entered the Australian culture regardless of ethnic origin or any other culture they share. Describing seventh generation Australians as 'Anglo' or 'Irish' is close to meaningless. At that distance, everyone is a mixture, and affection for Britain or Ireland usually owes more to personality than ethnicity. Using hyphens to describe Australians whose parents spoke another language at home is more understandable yet may give a misleading impression of ambivalence about Australia.

On both sides of the constitutional argument – either in hope or in fear – protagonists take for granted a type of ethnic determinism which they would strive to overcome in any other context. As home to people born in virtually every country on earth, Australians can hardly afford to let ethnicity become a determining factor in domestic politics. Whether the English love the Queen – or the Irish hate her; whether the New Zealanders love England – or the French the opposite, is beside the point. All that counts, from an Australian point of view, is the attitude of Australians.

As the only practical method of keeping politics out of the top job and providing an impartial referee at the apex of our system of government, there are advantages to our system which do not require particular ethnicity for their appreciation. Scepticism towards politicians, for instance, seems to have become a universal characteristic, equally ingrained in old and new Australians. So why should anyone conclude that future waves of 'ethnic' voters will 'inevitably' support a republic which politicises the head of state?

The oft-heard claim that Australia can never be truly free with a British monarch on the Australian throne is, perhaps, the sorriest argument in the republican arsenal because it ignores Australia's history and implicitly denigrates everything Australia has achieved up till now.

An Australian identity is only a few months younger, it seems, than settlement itself. Almost from the beginning, Australia had its own distinctive outlook. Within a few years, the native-born (or 'currency' lads and lasses as they became known) saw themselves as more self-reliant, down-to-earth and ready-to-turn-their-hands-to-anything than their British-born (or 'sterling') fellow colonists.

In 1827, the surgeon and pastoralist Peter Cunningham described the 'currency' children as honest, sober and mild-tempered, as well as taller and healthier than their British counterparts [Blainey p. 33]. Another settler of the period wrote:

> Though I myself glory, and shall die glorying in the name of *Englishman*, yet my children glory in another name. To be *Australian* is their signal word...
>
> **Blainey, p. 34**

Australia's first great patriot, William Charles Wentworth, was the son of a convict mother and a father who had left England under a cloud. As an explorer of the Blue Mountains, Wentworth was already a local hero when he went to Cambridge. His entry in the university poetry competition proclaimed that Australia floats 'with Flag unfurled, a new Britannia in another world'. As if to prove that we had already developed a style of debate no less rugged than the landscape, Charles Harpur wrote a parody claiming that Australia was 'a barbarous Britain under other skies' spreading 'with Flag unfurled, all thy worst features through a wider world' [Partington, p. 192].

By the 1830s, Australia was already proving the world's greatest ever exercise in penal rehabilitation. Many of the colony's leading citizens were ex-convicts – redeemed by opportunity and hard work – and the children of convicts largely turned out to be exemplary citizens. In the 1840s, the now respectable colonists prevailed over London to force the abolition of transportation. In 1855, thanks to further local agitation, New South Wales was granted responsible self-government and the other colonies shortly followed suit. Within scarcely half a century of settled existence, Australia was as politically sophisticated as the Canadians, and had achieved a higher level of political independence than the American colonies prior to the Revolutionary War.

In 1856, 95% of Sydney men could vote. By this time, Australia was the world's most thorough-going democracy. In NSW and Victoria, Aborigines had the right to vote – unlike America's still-to-be-emancipated slaves. Nine tenths of our population enjoyed universal manhood suffrage – 50 years in advance of England. Politicians had to stand for re-election every three years – unlike France which had six year terms and a heavily censored press.

By the 1890s, Australia had the world's highest standard of living. Compared to Britons, Australians were better housed and better fed, had more time off and more money in their pockets. Compared to America, Australia lacked extremes of wealth and poverty, some of the more vicious forms of racism, and extensive industrial slums.

A people, a spirit and a fellowship

In 1882, says Elaine Thompson, refuting the canard that 'Australia was a cultural desert', Britain had one newspaper for every 18,000 people – compared to one for just under 6000 people in Victoria [*Sydney Morning Herald*, 10 June, 1995]. By the 1890s, Australia had its own artistic tradition, developed by the Heidelberg school; its own literature, in the poetry of Banjo Patterson and Henry Lawson; its own songs, *Waltzing Matilda* and *Advance Australia Fair*; its own inventions: the stump jump plough, Sunshine harvester, and box kite; its own mythology about democracy, human rights, persecution and the Eureka Stockade; and its own folk heroes such as Ned Kelly. In America, the secret ballot was known as the 'Australian ballot' because it was first practised here and Australia was the first country to give women the vote 30 years in advance of Britain.

By the 1890s, says Blainey:

Australia was becoming more than just a land to which people came hoping to find as much as possible of the land they had left behind. It was becoming a people, a spirit and sometimes a fellowship, a tale of failures and achievement. Some disliked to their dying day the landscape, the glaring heat and light but still did not wish to return to their first homeland. Others rejoiced in almost everything Australian and began in the 1890s to nourish the idea that it was the Australian environment and especially the bush which made Australians a different people.

Blainey, p. 106

Participation in two world wars honed Australians' sense of being unique. In World War One, Australians were plucky fighters but sloppy saluters. Alone among the nations, the Australian army did not employ conscription nor shoot deserters. The legend of Simpson and his donkey suggested to generations of Australian school children that, even in war, it was better to preserve life than to take it. Not only did Australians in World War Two secure the first military victory over Japan at Milne Bay – but, along the Burma Railway, won a moral victory that was even more important: to their guards' amazement, always carrying the wounded and sick with them, attempting to keep officers and men together, and insisting that cooks eat last.

With post-war immigration, Australia opened its doors to the 'poor, huddled masses' of war-torn Europe in proportions unrivalled by anyone else. And they were engaged on great public works such as the Snowy Mountains Scheme in an exercise in material and communal nation-building. Of course, Australia's treatment of migrants was far from perfect – just as our treatment of Aborigines had been far from perfect. But Arthur Calwell's cruel jest over the operation of the Immigration Restriction Act that 'two wongs don't make a white' was no more representative of Australian attitudes than Gough Whitlam's later denunciation of boat people as 'fucking yellow Balts'.

Although Federation did not, in fact, mark complete and final legal independence, it marked our beginning as an organised national entity. Before 1901, Australia was a geographical entity, a state of mind, a distinctive sub-group of the English-speaking community – but it was not an extant national entity. In that sense, 1901 is as much a milestone to Australians as 1776 is to Americans, and Federation should be as important to us as the Declaration of Independence is to them.

In 1901, Australians saw themselves as part of the British Empire. But we were a free and self-governing part of an Empire which was an association of choice. In those days, there was no contradiction between being 'British' and being 'Australian'. For Australians, 'Britishness' did not mean wearing bowler hats to work or speaking with fruity accents. It meant belonging to a mutual self-help society bound together by ties of trade and defence in the strongest alliance between different nations the world had ever seen. It meant participation in a supra-national association with common bonds, a common language, and the common law system – the finest and fairest yet evolved.

In the eyes of most Australians, the British Empire was unlike any that had gone before. The Empires of the Assyrians, the Romans and even the Greeks had been built on conquest and exploitation but the bits of pink on the world's map were linked by shared values as much as by shared interests. When the news came across the wires that Britain had declared war on Germany in 1914, crowds cheered outside the Sydney GPO and Labor Leader Andrew Fisher declared that Australia would stand by the Mother Country to the last man and the last shilling.

Of course, imperial good faith was not always self-evident to Australians with an affinity for Ireland – but most of these combined love of Ireland with an appreciation of British civic virtues. Tom Keneally has claimed that his grandfather believed Queen Victoria wore high collars to hide syphilitic sores on her neck [Partington, p. X] – but most of the time, most Irish Australians had other things on their minds.

The early *Bulletin* thundered against 'the worm-eaten lie of the divine right of kings to murder peasants, but few Australians felt any instinctive hostility to Britain itself. If the British were ever in the wrong, it was because they had failed to match the ideals which Britons and Australians had in common. Although Archbishop Mannix misjudged the Great War as a 'sordid trade war' rather than an epic struggle for freedom, that did not stop Catholics enlisting at the same rate as their countrymen.

It is important to recall the atmospherics of those times – not to indulge in nostalgia for what was and what can never be again, nor to reproach our forbears for being unlike ourselves – but to savour the spirit which has made us. The country which donned uniform in 1914 and again in 1939 was not populated by men from Mars but by our fathers and grandfathers and national pride demands an acknowledgment of their values.

The greatest, most powerful and most splendid of nations
Australians of the Federation era looked and sounded different from Britons. We already had our own poets, our own writers, our own heroes and our own myths. A visiting Englishman captured the dreams of late Victorian Australians:

> With a population of a hundred millions, having in their veins the best and most vigorous blood of these islands, blending in themselves all the best qualities of the English, Scotch and Irish people, inheriting the material, intellectual and moral triumphs of European civilisation, living in a country the resources of which are boundless, and under skies such as poets in their dreams have seen bending over the islands of the blessed, Australia, a hundred years hence, will become one of the greatest, most powerful and most splendid of nations. These are the prophecies and hopes on which the more ardent and generous of the young Australians delight to dwell.

> **Blainey, p. 95**

In the Federation era, and for several decades afterwards, we were Australian *and* British because it suited us to be that way. But when it did not, we were just Australian. In 1882, the Queensland Government wanted to stop a German take-over of New Guinea. When London failed to act, Brisbane did. Queensland's annexation of Papua was subsequently over-ruled, but Australians got what they wanted – the Union Jack flying on both sides of the Torres Strait.

The Gallipoli Campaign strongly reinforced Australia's sense of self – even as Australians served within large imperial formations. As Charles Bean said: 'It rises as it will always rise, above the mists of ages, a monument to great hearted men – and for their nation a possession forever'. Australia's contribution to World War One: nearly 10% of a population of just 4 million serving overseas, 60,000 dead, over the war's full course, the highest casualty rate of the British Empire and the Anzac Corps under General Monash playing a decisive role in halting and rolling back the last big German push, earned Australia an individual place at the Versailles Peace Conference.

At Versailles, Prime Minister Billy Hughes successfully argued for Australian administration of the captured German territory in northern New Guinea, even enunciating what sounded very much like the beginnings of an Australian 'Monroe Doctrine' in the South Pacific. Hughes and subsequent prime ministers trenchantly opposed the Treaty of Washington, which gave Japan the right to build a navy three-fifths the size of Britain's, and – rebuffed – pushed for the speedy construction of the Singapore bastion which, they hoped, would secure Australia's northern defences.

With hindsight's 20/20 vision, the 'Singapore strategy' looks disastrously misconceived. These days, reliance on the Empire is often portrayed as a form of adolescent dependence. Yet the base at Singapore was necessary to secure Britain's involvement in the defence of Australia – and enmeshing great powers on one's own side is basic common sense.

In an era of big power conflict in our own region, Australia's cultivation of 'great and powerful friends' was no more dishonourable than the French construction of an Entente Cordiale to check the Kaiser's Germany nor, for that matter, Churchill's attempt to enlist Stalin in the war against Hitler. When independence is at stake, well-led nations find their allies where they may – and so much the better if those allies are bound by ties of kinship and common culture as well as self-interest.

Prime ministers from Hughes to Menzies invoked the rhetoric of 'kith and kin' but it was Australia they were trying to protect. Two days after the fall of Singapore, John Curtin actually addressed the nation as 'the sons and daughters of Britishers'. At the time, Curtin's 'look to America' speech was a statement of the obvious. It did not mark a change in Australia's self-understanding nor a break in our relations with the 'mother country' – a fact Curtin emphasised when he appointed the King's brother as Governor-General and Chifley confirmed when he asked Lord Mountbatten to succeed the Duke of Gloucester at Yarralumla [Atkinson, p. 20]. Menzies' 1939 announcement that, as a result of Britain's declaration of war, 'Australia is also at war', may now sound quaint but there was (understandably) little criticism at the time and his earlier comment that the 'far east' was really Australia's 'near north' shows whose defence was his chief concern.

Unlike Paul Keating, Bob Hawke (who declared his personal republicanism in the 1979 Boyer Lectures) never mixed up republicanism with anti-British prejudice. In 1989, speaking of the relationship between Australia and Britain, Hawke declared that 'our shared language and culture, the strong bonds of history and of kinship, our familiar institutions of political, economic, legal and academic life' mean that (passport queues at Heathrow notwithstanding) Australians in the UK 'can never arrive as strangers'. By contrast, Keating claimed that 'Australia's interests and Britain's interests are often very different – and even fundamentally opposed' [*Australian Financial Review*, 9 November, 1995] despite the UK's support for Australian initiatives on the Uruguay Round, human rights, arms control and UN reform. But then, even Humphrey McQueen once noted that the former Prime Minister had exposed himself to ridicule 'by putting his own Irish prejudices on paper' [*Australian*, 16 June, 1997].

Cultural evolution writ small

The street I live in is called Lady Davidson Circuit – because it runs along the edge of a large bushland park originally named after the wife of an imperial dignitary. A few years ago, the park was incorporated into a larger area with an Aboriginal name but the street name stayed the same. This is a homely example of cultural evolution writ small. As Australia's independent history lengthens, what is 'British' diminishes and what is 'Australian' increases. Yet over time, what was once 'British' becomes incorporated into what is now Australian.

Cricket, rugby and soccer are no longer English games even though they originated in England, had their rules codified there and for many years were administered from London. Shakespeare is not an English possession although he spent his whole life in England. His work is part of the common heritage of Western civilisation.

Blainey has contrasted the present 'black armband' view with an earlier 'three cheers' conception of Australian history. Despite the enormities perpetrated against Aborigines and ingrained cultural insensitivities towards minorities, Australia's history gives more grounds for pride than shame. In any event, our history can be denied but not undone. For better and for worse, it has made modern Australia.

For some of its leaders, republicanism can seem part of a wider rejection of tradition. Writing in the late '50s, when he was 'a boy from the suburbs', Donald Horne eulogised the poetry of

A.D. Hope as on the grounds that it was 'un-Australian' [*Good Weekend,* 22 May, 1993]. Horne says that this no more represented his mature outlook than his primary school oration celebrating the achievements of the British Empire. Although Horne has been an important chronicler of contemporary Australia, he has rarely liked what he saw and the 'lucky country' tag, which Australians cheerfully took at face value, was conceived as a kind of lament.

Tom Keneally has talked about the time, just a few years ago, when it was 'every writer's sacred duty to be alienated by Australia – to be a European soul descended into this terrible place' [*Good Weekend,* 26 June, 1993]. Perhaps this was a passing phase, like his one-time insistence on singing *God Save the Queen,* and not *Hail Queen of Heaven,* before the seminary play. At his best, Keneally can speaking movingly of republicanism as an act of homage to our British past yet at other times he sounds like an over-excited tourist in a Dublin pub.

Horne and Keneally are the patriarchs of Australian republicanism but Paul Keating made it front page news. Despite his pivotal role, there is no record that Keating had ever evinced any republican enthusiasm prior to 1992. Once awakened, Keating's republican passions expressed themselves as antagonism to Britain, contempt for his political opponents, and impatience with the past – rather than any great affection for the country he apparently described as the 'arse end of the earth'. Keating was undoubtedly an Australian patriot but there was a dark side to his fervour. He sometimes gave the impression that his affection for the country did not extend to very many individual Australians (whom he once described as 'yobs with cans in their hands').

The post-modern republic

Atkinson has described the 'post-modern' republic as a 'campaign against the core culture' in which 'variety will replace unity and superficiality will flourish instead of depth'. For many republicans, he says, 'the very emptiness of the republican idea is part of its charm... (and) the emotional foundation of the republic is a recollection of an absence that can appeal to everyone' [Atkinson, p. 117]. It is an appeal to abolish history, its burdens and its foibles.

In April 1994, the Singaporean elder statesmen Lee Kuan Yew scoffed at claims that becoming a republic would enhance Australia's image in Asia. But if, as republicans often claim, Asians think of Australia as still tied to Britain, they can hardly be blamed – after all, Keating told them exactly that. The problem with telling foreign audiences that Australia is seeking full independence by becoming a republic is the inference that Australia is not fully independent now. Pretending that Australia will never be able to succeed until it becomes a republic suggests that, up till now, everything that happened here was provincial, second rate, and only worth taking seriously if it prefigured a republic.

Imre Salusinszky has identified three strands in contemporary republicanism:

> If you're part of the Irish crowd, republicanism provides a displaced version of the war against perfidious Albion... At the University of Melbourne I was taught by men who passionately supported the transformation of Northern Ireland into a society where it would be impossible to get divorced, buy contraceptives or procure abortions for girlfriends – activities they themselves pursued to a degree way beyond the national average.
>
> Then again, if you're a Whitlam era dinosaur... you can use republicanism to refocus attention on the unspeakable things that were done to you in November 1975...
>
> Meanwhile, if you are a prime minister who has lost interest in economic reform and is about to throw in the towel and just raise taxes, republicanism creates the illusion of still having a reformist agenda.

Australian Financial Review, **23 December, 1994**

Republicanism was Keating's way of keeping faith with Gough Whitlam while scorning Labor's former economic policy. Indeed, Horne has described Keating's 'big picture' as a 'few snapshots, enlarged, from the Whitlam age' [*Sydney Morning Herald*, 11 November, 1995]. Whitlam, of course, had promoted himself as the 'young green tree' in contrast to Menzies' 'old dead tree'. Although Whitlam has said that he himself only became a republican after his dismissal, his time was a significant prelude to the current argument insofar as constantly attacking what went before has become a way of boosting what was to come.

In politics, no-one wins unless someone else loses. Perhaps any movement led by politicians will involve an exaggerated 'them and us' mentality and an abundance of false triumphalism. 'We' are all-wise, all-good, all-powerful – 'they' are all-wrong, all-bad, all-doomed. With his wit, urbanity and massive subsidies to the arts, Whitlam won the allegiance of the opinion-forming elite. For thinkers of the standing of Patrick White and Manning Clark, it would not be unfair to say that the years before and after 1972 were the years before and after the coming of enlightenment.

Guilt about treatment of the Aborigines; an assumption that others are right and Australians are wrong; hope for the future – but only to the extent that it is different from the past; and uncritical admiration for foreigners – as long as they're not the foreigners we used to admire – are still part of the modern Australian zeitgeist, notwithstanding the election of the Howard Government. Keating's description of the Menzies era as Australia's Rip Van Winkle experience is pure Whitlam (or perhaps, as Graeme Campbell once said, 'comic book Manning Clark'). It is not really surprising that a politician dedicated to destroying what he saw as Menzies' economic legacy would subsequently turn his attention to Menzies' emotional and constitutional attachments.

'I did but see her passing by and yet I love her till I die'. Menzies' gushing welcome to an embarrassed young Queen now sounds off-putting – even servile. It seems as anachronistic as photographs of the ex-Prime Minister in the ceremonial uniform of the Lord Warden of the Cinque Ports yet three decades ago it captured the feelings of many Australians. These days, cringing adulation is more likely to be reserved for Labor politicians – such as Jacki Weaver's comment, at the 1996 'Artists for Labor' rally: 'Paul, you'll never know how much you are loved'.

Cultural engineering

For most people who tell pollsters that they support the idea, republicanism is simply an expression of Australian patriotism. But to many of its leading adherents, republicanism is about changing Australia's identity, not celebrating it. A distinguished historian, the late Professor Austin Gough accused Keating of engaging in 'cultural engineering' reminiscent of the former Soviet Union, in which the Government creates a new social order and a new model citizen. Gough claimed that the arts community had duly responded:

> Like a Soviet style artists and writers union. The fawning on Keating has been astonishing, unprecedented in Australian cultural history. Some of the more excited representatives of theatres, galleries and publishing houses seem on the verge of hailing the (then) Prime Minister as Great Guide and Teacher or Beloved Elder Brother.
>
> *Weekend Australian,* **29-30 April, 1995**

For instance, on his appointment in 1994, the General Manager of the Australia Council described political commitment as part of his job.

> The arts industry as a whole, believes that we are more than capable of holding our own on the world stage. The unfortunate reality is that there is still a sense of outside control even if that control is only

psychological. It must be broken in order for artists to express themselves fully as artists. I cannot believe that we could go into the new millennium still tied to England...

Artforce, **September, 1994**

In the sense that republicanism existed long before Keating was born, continues to exist after his political demise, and has adherents of greater moral and intellectual weight, the current debate is no longer about 'Keating's republic'. But Keating was at once the best friend and the worst enemy of an Australian republic and Australian republicanism still carries the 'we are giants standing on the shoulders of pygmies' ambience which Keating created.

The argument that Australia cannot be itself except as a republic may turn out to be self-defeating, akin to telling someone: 'you'll only be any good if you stop being who you are'. Every time republicanism is preached as an instant cure for getting on with Asia to winning medals at the Olympics, the more messianic republicans seem and the more likely Australians will react with scepticism.

If becoming a republic is the essential pre-condition for Australia to be unique and distinctive, the achievements of pre-republican Australia are devalued. The cattle kings were not pioneers, just merchants. The Anzacs were not patriots, just imperialists – or acting under a delusion of freedom and independence. Those who made the Snowy Mountains scheme were not nation-builders at all, just plumbers and electricians with notions above their station.

To persuade people to make the change, republicans must over-state its potential rewards but in doing so they risk understating Australia's existing achievements. Republicans are in the position of salesmen trying to sign up new customers. They need to be careful lest voters feel insulted. After all, few sales are secured by rubbishing the competition, especially if that is what the potential customer has been buying for years.

So long as it depends upon belittling the past, republicanism is unlikely to succeed. Republicanism must seem like the fulfilment and completion of Australia's destiny, not a rejection of its heritage. If Australia is ever to become a republic, it should be an act of completion, not rejection. It should be a renewal – rather than a re-shaping – of Australia's national identity.

Tom Keneally sometimes says that becoming a republic is like leaving home, the final step to adulthood. If so, most republicans seem intent on slamming the door on the way out. In the real world, 'leaving home' is seldom accomplished without tears and recriminations and, so far, becoming a republic looks more like a child attempting to get a divorce from his parents.

The 'cure-all' republic

If becoming a republic is inevitable, why do republicans so consistently want to force the pace? Because, in fact, republicanism has no more inevitability than Australia winning the Ashes. Marxism was the latest political movement to proclaim inevitability – yet the dictatorship of the proletariat has itself been consigned to the dustbin of history. The 'inevitable republic' is not the completion of Australia's destiny. It is a rhetorical trick masking an invitation to join a bandwagon.

Why should Australia develop a constitutional herd instinct? The fact that monarchy is an ancient institution is hardly reason to change. After all, this is an age which has rightly discovered the value of heritage. Australia's complete independence from Britain no more demands changing our Constitution than it requires changing our language.

A passage from Dr Brendan Nelson's 1995 Australia Day speech evokes both the sense that becoming a republic is a forgone conclusion plus the sense that it might always seem more trouble than it's worth:

> I didn't feel strongly one way or the other about a republic until I read the profile interview with a 99 year old man that had landed on the beaches of Gallipoli, published in the Melbourne *Age* on April 24, 1993. Half way through the interview he was reported as saying that 'I'm glad I will be dead soon'. Even with the recent push for euthanasia, you don't find too many people saying that. I went on to read that he was glad that he would be dead soon because he didn't want to be alive 'when Australia became a republic and the flag was changed'. He said that he had seen too many of his young friends die for what we now have.

Regardless of the size of opinion poll majorities for a republic, for the conceivable future at least there will be millions of Australians for whom becoming a republic would involve a wrenching sense of loss. Despite the Royal Family's problems and the extent of media barracking, support for a republic seems stuck at about 50% (of which a substantial proportion is only 'partly in favour').

The Morgan organisation began polling Australians' attitudes towards the monarchy in 1953. Support for the Monarchy began at 77% and oscillated around 60% from then until 1988. In July 1991, after Prince Charles' marriage problems had become known and after the ALP National Conference had declared its support for a republic by 2001, support for the monarchy was 56%. By March 1992, after the Prime Minister had attacked the Flag and the British, support dropped to 49% and then to just 38% in April 1993, after the re-elected Prime Minister asked the Turnbull Committee to prepare a republican blueprint. But in December 1993, after the opponents of a republic had begun their counterattack, support for the monarchy returned to 48% while support for a 'US-style republic' had dropped to 44%. Support for a republic peaked at 50% in November 1994 (but actually fell to 47% at the time of the Keating republican statement) before peaking again at 53% in the aftermath of the death of Princess Diana.

Newspoll began tracking support for a republic in 1987. Beginning at under 21%, it had risen to 34% by June 1991. In February 1992, it reached 44%, dropped back to 41% in May before hitting 46% in April 1993 after the Keating election win. In September 1993, it dropped back to 39% and took a year to rise again to 42% in November 1994 (prompting the exasperated headline from one pro-republican newspaper 'republic support slow to grow'), 47% in March 1995, 50% in June 1995, after the Keating announcement and 54% after the death of Princess Diana [*Australian*, 10 September, 1997].

The problem with polls

The fundamental difficulty with all such poll results is that they measure support for the republican principle – not for any particular republican practice. In August 1994 – when support for the republican principle was 45% – support for a republic where the president was elected by Parliament slumped to 32%, AGB McNair found. In January 1995 – when support for the republican principle had risen to 52% – only 40% of the electorate would support (and 48% would oppose) a republic where the president was elected by Parliament.

From the beginning, polls have recorded very high support for the proposition that – if Australia is to become a republic – the president should be directly elected by the people. Between February 1994 and January 1995, AGB McNair recorded support for popular election of a president fluctuating between 86% and 91%. Newspoll put support for popular election at 79% in July 1993, 78% in March 1995 and 74% after Keating's statement. In June 1996, the Morgan Poll put support for a popularly elected president at 74% with just 20% supporting a form of parliament-ary election. Yet a directly elected president is the constitutional change nearly all leading republicans reject because they admit that a president with the moral authority of a personal mandate could soon create deadlock between Yarralumla and the Lodge.

Poll findings that the young are more likely to back a republic fuel the belief in republican inevitability. Yet as Goot has pointed out, the young who were more likely to favour a republic in the 1950s had become the middle-aged who were more likely to favour the monarchy in the 1980s. Because the underlying level of support for the monarchy was relatively constant over many years, Goot concluded that each generation of young republicans tended to become the next generation of middle-aged monarchists.

Bob Hawke has consistently argued – because of the Queen's high public standing – that an Australian republic should wait until the end of the present reign. This, of course, could be a generation away. That way, says Hawke, the generations to whom it meant a great deal will be spared the pain of cutting what they perceive to be a link with Britain.

Letting the over 55s die off

Hawke's view assumes that becoming a republic is mostly a matter of letting the over-55s die off. Some polls actually show support for a republic highest amongst those aged from 35 to 50. For instance, the September 1997 Newspoll showed that 38% of 35 to 49 year olds (but just 32% of 18 to 34 year olds) were 'strongly in favour' of becoming a republic. Similarly 27% of youngsters (but only 24% of the middle aged) were opposed to a republic [*Australian*, 10 September, 1997].

Amongst those aged under 35, support for the Crown is not especially weak – and neither is support for a republic partic-ularly strong. One survey of 300 16 to 17 year olds reportedly

revealed 'the unanimous expectation of a republic' [*Australian,* 5 August, 1996]. Such a survey probably reveals more about youngsters' desire to conform than their real views. In fact, young Australians seem to be uncommitted and many could go either way.

In 1993, during an SBS television program which attempted to put the Constitution on trial, 'jurors' burst into tears and threw glasses of water at each other [*Australian,* 30 September, 1993]. When the nude sculpture, 'Down by the Lake with Liz and Phil' was displayed, fisticuffs erupted as a policeman who had seven times sworn an oath of allegiance to the Queen tried to defend her dignity [*Sydney Morning Herald,* 17 April, 1995].

As every politician sooner or later finds out, the anger of 'losers' nearly always outweighs the gratitude of 'winners'. A republic is something which even its staunchest supporters have hitherto been able to live without. By contrast, our existing Constitution has been taken for granted by millions who cannot be counted upon to appreciate its removal, however undemonstrative they might be now.

As Michael Kirby has said:

> Democracy works best when it respects the opinion of diverse groups in all parts of the population, not just the majority.

Quadrant, **September 1993**

One way of institutionalising a 'them-and-us' mentality is to insist on changes which some groups simply cannot accept. Democracy does not mean the right of a majority to humiliate a minority, so republicans (even in the event of substantial poll support for a republic) need to be careful lest change leaves millions of Australians permanently embittered.

Civilised governments, for instance, would not dream of interfering with the wearing of turbans or veils – no matter what percentage of the population find such things incomprehensible or not to their taste – because these practices are sacred to some and cause no harm to anyone else. Republicans invariably claim that change will make no practical difference to the way Australia works. Even if it is just a question of symbols – the constitutional equivalent of turbans and veils – substantial opinion poll majorities in favour of a republic would not justify change if its opponents were likely to feel permanently left out.

Polls can measure the 'quantity' – but not the 'quality' – of popular feeling. Gauging the depth of commitment requires much more than asking whether people feel 'strongly' or 'partly' either way. One guide is AGB McNair's finding in October 1993 and again in August 1994, that 55 and 66% respectively thought that any move to a republic would cause 'a lot' or 'some' social division. Another indicator is Bob Hawke's view, throughout his prime ministership, that republicanism was 'too hot to handle'.

To defeat a referendum proposal, supporters of the status quo do not have to persuade people that our existing constitutional arrangement is perfect – just that it is better than the alternative. By contrast, if the issue ever comes to the constitutional crunch, republicans are likely to divide into those who want to change virtually everything and those who want to change practically nothing.

When faced with the Keating Republic, some republicans adopted the position of St Augustine: 'give me a republic – but not yet'. One lifelong republican, the poet Les Murray, has said that Australians will not vote for a republic unless they trust it and 'they sure can't trust the one they are being offered at the moment' [*Australian*, 20 September, 1993]. Ex-Victorian Premier Joan Kirner has said that the worst result of the republican push would be a series of referendum campaigns:

> ... dominated by politicians slugging it out head-to-head. We all know that would end in a 'no' vote on every proposal.
>
> *Australian*, **11 August, 1994**

Labor has had its fair share of splits on this issue. Hawke persistently attacked his successor for rushing the pace. 'There are many more important things to get your knickers in a knot about than get excited about the republican issue' is a typical Hawke comment [*Sun-Herald*, 2 April, 1995]. At the 1994 ALP National Conference, President Barry Jones chided Keating for keeping the voting public in the dark. 'It is a mystery to me why we haven't explained what we want already'. The problem, he said, was the 'top down' approach adopted by the Keating Government. 'Where is the Party in all this. Even more important, where is the community?' [AAP, 26 September, 1994].

One of the clearest demonstrations of the difficulties republicans face, was the Constitutional Centenary Foundation's Conference in May 1995. It was supposed to craft the questions which might be put to Australians in a referendum to become a republic but became bogged down on all the essential points. Delegates were split on whether an indicative plebiscite should be held to gauge voters' feeling about choosing a head of state or the state of the reserve powers [*Australian Financial Review*, 9 May, 1995]. Malcolm Turnbull was hissed by his fellow delegates for hogging the microphone, past the expiry of his speaking time, to insist that his proposal for an appointed president be put to a vote ahead of everything else.

A subsequent CCF invitation-only conference, in Adelaide in April 1997, attempted to 'identify the principles on which Australian government should be based as the nation and the Constitution move into their second century'. The conference supported: more scope for initiating referendums, plain English in constitution-writing, compulsory voting, recognition of indigenous law, access to justice for all regardless of means, the provision of interpreters to non-English speaking litigants, and civics education taking into account 'the linguistic and cultural diversity in Australia'. The conference concluded that 'the monarch of the United Kingdom will cease to be Australia's head of state who will be an Australian citizen chosen by Australians' – but P.P. McGuinness (who was one of the participants) rather spoiled the party by pointing out that if you invite republican zealots you get a republican outcome [*Sydney Morning Herald*, 26 April, 1997].

Historically, Australian republicanism has been a radical cause. Now that it has become an establishment cause – backed by former prime ministers, some State Premiers and most major newspapers – leading republicans say that only the letterhead at Yarralumla need change. What is the point of change, millions will ask, if it does not actually mean anything? Why should a republic help, some will say, when so few other 'reform' schemes have? And what's the rush, others will say, if it is bound to happen sooner or later anyway?

From the beginning of the current debate, there has been considerable tension between those for whom republicanism symbolises radical change and those for whom republicanism is merely symbolic. At times, Malcolm Turnbull has described becoming a republic as the 'first step in a journey of a thousand leagues' or as a 'steel wheel clattering down the cobbled street of our national consciousness' which will strike the sparks necessary for 'more and greater reforms in the future' [*AM*, 17 May, 1995]. At other times, he has attacked linking other causes to republicanism – lest it strike voters as the Trojan horse for radical change.

Republicans who, in other respects, support the Westminster system may oppose a republic with an elected president because of the potential to politicise the role of head of state. Those without faith in the existing system may refuse to support a republic which gives politicians the power to choose the effective as well as the nominal head of state. Labor voters may resent a proposed system which, by preserving the head of state's existing powers, posthumously endorses Sir John Kerr's decision to sack Gough Whitlam. Liberal voters, regardless of how they feel about the Queen, may reject a republic where the head of state's role is substantially changed. In any event, the harder the issue is fought, the more divisive and unnecessary becoming a republic is likely to seem.

Force of habit is not the only reason why countries maintain a monarchy. Constitutional monarchy has strong arguments in its favour – over and above 'why bother to change'. The assertion that a republic is 'inevitable' assumes that nothing can replace a fast-fading sense of 'Britishness'. It implies that the 'punters' are incapable of finding new reasons to support old institutions.

'Inevitable' means 'not yet'

In fact, proclaiming inevitability may be a way of genuflecting to republican sentiment without embracing republican ideas. 'It's inevitable' might often mean 'not yet'. In the wake of Keating's republican statement, the one convinced republican among Liberal Leaders, NSW Opposition Leader Peter Collins, strongly backed Howard's alternative of the People's Convention but vehemently opposed the NSW Labor Government's proposal to remove the Crown from State oaths – on the grounds that, prior to the establishment of a republic, it would be premature, divisive and disrespectful to the Queen.

Collins, of course, remains a strong supporter of Australia becoming a republic. But his criticism of Keating and Carr shows the difficulty of fundamental change under an adversarial system of politics. In the unlikely event that the Federal Liberal Party turned republican, the ALP might well find significant objections to the specifics of a proposal (much as the New Zealand Labour leader did when Jim Bolger announced his support for a republic). The adversarial system does not preclude co-operation in a good cause (such as the wartime Advisory Council), but it guarantees that even a genuine consensus will be subject to critical scrutiny.

In the governor-general versus president debate, with strong emotional attachments on either side of the argument and the 'opposition-for-opposition's sake' dynamic inherent in a two party system, the question may one day be asked not: 'When will a republic come about?' but: 'Why did anyone ever think it was inevitable?'.

CHAPTER NINE

The changing Crown

S OME argue that the Crown is not at the core of the Australian ethos. In some respects, with its associations of pomp and panoply, it sits oddly with the Australian self-image. The Crown is not now – and probably never has been – at the forefront of the Australian consciousness but it is part of our cultural furniture as well as our legal structure. The Crown is no more 'foreign' to Australia than cricket and Shakespeare and when he described the Australian Crown as a 'bunyip monarchy', Alan Atkinson was making a point about its local flavour as much as its mythic nature.

The cities of Sydney and Melbourne are named after Ministers of the Crown. Adelaide is named after William IV's consort. The State of Victoria is named after the Queen Empress as is Queensland, of course. Every politician, judge, and military officer has sworn allegiance to the Crown. So has every new citizen until 1994. The crown may have disappeared from most mail boxes but it remains on the crests of vast numbers of Australian institutions from the RSL badge to the insignia of the Order of Australia. Despite the best efforts of the Keating Government, many schools, clubs and Government offices still have a picture of the Queen on their walls.

Sick Australians are likely to attend a 'Royal' hospital. Sports followers may visit a 'Royal' race track, golf course or sailing club. Many country towns boast a 'Royal' hotel. With charters ranging from the protection of animals to the provision of air ambulances, any number of charitable institutions testify to the Crown's place in the sub-text of Australian life.

A few clubs aside, there is nothing pretentious or 'un-Australian' about any of these institutions. Their members and beneficiaries don't wear the royal badge with any self-conscious importance. Their pride is in themselves not in their connections. Nevertheless, the royal tag is a sign of recognition which, if they ever thought about it, few would want taken away.

To Australians of the wartime generation, the Crown will always symbolise the grit of a far-flung people united in a struggle against tyranny. For Australians over 30, there would be few who lack royal memories, stretching from the 1954 Royal Tour (which is thought to have been watched by 75% of Australians – Atkinson, p. 86) to the Bicentenary celebrations on Sydney Harbour when Prince Charles' speech captured the spirit of the day far better than those of the Prime Minister or Premier.

In the same week in 1995 that the NSW Premier announced his intention to delete all reference to the Crown from oaths of office, hundreds of delegates to the RSL State Conference personally re-pledged their allegiance to the Queen and the students of North Balgowlah Primary School marked the school's 40th birthday by dressing up as Captain Cook, Florence Nightingale and Queen Victoria to celebrate Empire Day.

Every day in Parliament, proclaimed republicans talk about 'Ministers of the Crown'. Their self-description is not 'tribune of the people' nor 'servant of the state', because, in our society, 'Minister of the Crown' denotes service, dignity, and restraint.

Perhaps it would not take 200 years for the 'Presidential Hotel', and 'State Prosecutor' to attain the same lustre as their monarchical equivalents, but – until they do – the honorifics of an Australian republic will seem emotionally threadbare.

As Bagehot said of the 19th century monarchy:

> It seems to order but it never seems to struggle. It is commonly hidden like a mystery, and is sometimes paraded like a pageant, but in neither case is it contentious. The nation is divided into parties but the Crown is of no party.

A human dimension to the State

The Crown gives authority a human dimension. Even in the Age of Big Government, the apparatus of the state is supposed to serve the Crown. As the master of the state and as the servant of the people, the Crown can be appealed to when the state does wrong. An illustration of this is the strong resistance to becoming a republic among many New Zealand Maoris. The Treaty of Waitangi, which guaranteed Maori rights to enjoyment of their land, was signed with Queen Victoria and not with the New Zealand Government. Symbolic protection is better than no protection at all and, for some Maori at least, the Crown has been a symbol of justice in a society which was not very fair.

If the Crown has been a reminder of good intentions, it can also be a reproach to bad. Oppressive regimes (such as the Fijian military government and the South African apartheid government) have treated the Crown as an obstacle to their plans. It has not saved the victims of persecution but it has symbolised the values which would have kept them free.

Some republicans profess outrage at the requirement that the monarch be an Anglican. Many aspects of the Act of Succession seem anachronistic today – but if they were likely to disbar the heir to the throne, doubtless they would be changed. It is possible to view the religious test as a sign of the Crown's ingrained bigotry but more sensible to see past the accidents of history to the Christian values which have been a constant leaven in our civilisation.

The monarch's position as Head of the Church of England makes her a symbol of religious commitment in a secular state. Prince Charles is said to prefer the title 'defender of faith'. At worst, this is harmless tradition. At best, it is a powerful reminder of enduring values that should transcend the 'them-and-us', 'what's-in-it-for-me', 'nothing-counts-except-the-bottom-line' approach that often threatens to dominate government and degrade contemporary society.

Even the low-key, short-on-ceremony aspect of the Crown in Australia points to values we forget at our peril. Sir William Deane lacks the pomp and panoply attending on the Crown at Westminster but the need for political leaders to transact business through the Governor-General's Executive Council is a reminder that ministers are not all-powerful. It is a sign of the long-standing checks and balances on executive power which Australia has made her own and improved upon.

In his autobiography, Barry Humphries talks of a schooldays meeting with the Australian composer Percy Grainger:

> I, a mere Melbourne schoolboy, had now shaken hands with the creator of *The Magic Flute*; for had not Percy shaken hands with Greig who had shaken hands with Liszt who had shaken hands with Beethoven who had shaken hands with Haydn, who had clasped the hand of Mozart.

Queen Elizabeth has seen nine British and nine Australian prime ministers come and go. When she came to the throne, Churchill was in Downing Street, Menzies was at the Lodge and Eisenhower was in the White House. De Gaulle had yet to establish the Fifth Republic. Even though she has been represented in that time by 11 Australian governors-general, the Crown represents a living link with an age of epic struggle and undeniable achievement. In an age when little is built to last, a Crown that can trace its lineage back 1,000 years is – next to the Papacy – the oldest continuing institution of Western civilisation. Perhaps this is the kind of anachronism Australia needs in order to prevent the complete triumph of Kentucky Fried Culture.

Living links

The United Nations contains nearly 200 republics but only about 20 monarchies. The Australian system makes us a highly refined member of a rather select club. Australia has a derivative crown, a written constitution and an acknowledgment, in the separate offices of monarch and governor-general, of the hereditary principle and the principle of merit. Becoming a republic would make us more constitutionally run-of-mill and the republican insistence on being 'uniquely Australian' sometimes seems more like a constitutional version of the urge to conform, like wanting to replace Australian Rules Football (which is unique to Australia) with soccer (which is virtually universal) as the national game.

One of the most curious features of modern republicanism – and one of its sharpest differences with earlier Australian expressions of republicanism – is its internationalist flavour. We are urged to change because other countries in our region are republics and because change will 'modernise' our image. Since when have Australians sweated on what other countries think of us, substituted a definite modern cringe for alleged sub-servience to Mother England, or craved to be like other countries rather than distinctively Australian?

There was a nasty, exclusionist side to the 1890s *Bulletin* republicans but there was no question of their faith in Australia and pride in Australia's achievements. By contrast, some modern republicans see change as an act of atonement to our neighbours in much the same way that some people justify Australia's immigration policy on the grounds that Asians will teach us how to work.

In terms of people's daily lives, removing the symbolism of the Crown would count far less than the already-under-way removal of other elements in the Federation compact, such as industrial arbitration and tariff protection. These were once fixtures in the Australian economic and social landscape and their erosion over the past two decades, while doubtless good for economic efficiency, has left many Australians feeling exposed to forces they cannot control. Becoming a republic may confirm Australians' suspicions that they live in an age where everything is disposable.

Even today, ideas about the monarchy are shaped by prejudice as much as fact. For instance, an official of the Australian Republican Movement wrote that the monarchy was a religiously bigoted, anti-Semitic, adulterous and archaic obscenity and that monarchists were a 'forelock-tugging, arse-licking, cringing, crawling group of Australians' (letter written by Executive Officer, Qld branch Australian Republican Movement, 14 March, 1994).

In fact, nearly 800 years of constitutional evolution have transformed the Crown. The medieval King of England was a prince-general with supreme power over his subjects. The modern Queen has trouble commanding her own family – a problem she shares with not a few Australians. Then, the Crown was the focus of power. Now, power resides with elected politicians.

People can inherit good looks, money, brains and a retinue – but not power itself – and the only hereditary public position is the one which no longer carries any political clout. It was not always so, of course. Prior to Magna Carta, in 1215, the

English monarch was an absolute ruler restrained only by his own conscience and the power of his rivals. But Magna Carta – which actually guaranteed the rights of nobles rather than commoners – was the beginning of constitutional government because the Crown acknowledged that its formal power was no longer limitless but subject to God and the law.

In the next century, Edward III needed Parliament's help to raise the taxes necessary to wage his long wars in France. Thus began the struggle between Crown and Parliament which culminated in the Glorious Revolution of 1688 and the English Bill of Rights. It encompassed a civil war, the execution of a king and a short-lived republic – 'the Commonwealth' – but at its end, the Crown understood that sovereignty depended upon the consent of the people while the people, insofar as it is possible to judge these things, had concluded that a monarch lent stability and restraint to the process of government.

As late as the 18th century, the King – and not the House of Commons – personally chose the Prime Minister yet the need to secure a parliamentary majority for raising taxes and passing laws meant that, by the 19th century, the 'King's First Minister' was actually responsible to parliament rather than the monarch.

In the middle of the last century, Bagehot declared that there were two dimensions to English Government: the Crown with its panoply of tradition and circumstance was 'dignified'; parliament, courts and cabinet were 'efficient'. The Crown was for show; the cabinet was for substance. Cabinet was for 'bread'; the Crown was for 'circuses'. The sovereignty of parliament was re-enforced by the 1909-1911 constitutional crisis in which King George V agreed to appoint as many peers as were necessary to ensure that the Government's money bills passed through the House of Lords and that the Lords could not block parliamentary reform.

Spoiled Sloane Rangers

Of course, being 'decorative' may actually be harder than being productive. The London mob did not like the way the widowed Queen Victoria withdrew from public life and used to stone her carriage in the 1860s. Edward VIII deeply scandalised many of his subjects by planning to marry a divorcee. The current crop of junior royals have seriously damaged the mystique of the Crown by looking like spoiled brats – but living up to public expectations is a problem for elected heads of state (and their families) too. Arguably, Watergate did at least as much damage to the presidency and the American psyche as the abdication crisis did to the monarchy and Britain's self-image. President Clinton's besetting problem is not any particular policy decision but the 'character' issue dogging someone who smoked dope but did not inhale and the perception of 'conduct unbecoming' in the president of a nation which takes values seriously.

Scandal in high places is nothing new. From King David on, rulers have made much of their opportunities to cuckold their subjects. Edward II was murdered, allegedly by red hot poker in the rectum, in a gruesome parody of his sexual tastes. When George I came to London, unable to speak a word of English, he left his wife imprisoned in a Hanoverian castle and brought with him two mistresses, one of whom was quickly nicknamed 'the maypole' because she was so thin, and the other 'the Elephant and Castle' after a London pub, because she was so fat. Royal mistresses have been taken for granted until very recent times. Modern royalty seems tame by comparison with George IV, who was paralytically drunk on his wedding day, abandoned his wife after she had borne a son and barred her from his coronation – or even with Edward VII, who was London's most notorious rake.

Media criticism is nothing new either. On the death of

George IV, an article in the London *Times* commented:

> There never was an individual less regretted by his fellow creatures...
> What heart has heaved one sob of unmercenary sorrow

Grainger and Jones, p. 153

In 1871, Gladstone noted that Queen Victoria's popularity levels 'go from bad to worse' and that anti-royal graffiti was daubed on railway stations [Grainger and Jones, p. 154].

A thousand years of constitutional evolution have changed the Crown from ruler to symbol, from politician-in-chief to national ornament. The British monarch's role has changed from scourge of subjects to protector of citizens. For the past century at least, the monarchy has been freedom's good friend. In South Africa and in Fiji, a republic gave freer rein to the enemies of freedom – not because the Queen was herself defending Indian shopkeepers or the residents of black townships but because the existence of the Crown had denied complete power to politicians. The Crown achieves its object simply by existing. The Crown does not need to act – it simply needs to be.

Hence, the republican claim, that a hereditary monarch makes as much sense as a hereditary cook, misunderstands the nature of the job. A monarch is not expected to be intelligent, witty, beautiful, skilful or powerful. To fulfil its role, the Crown simply has to exist. If the head of state's job is to avoid the slightest hint of partisanship, a hereditary constitutional monarch may best fit the bill.

The hereditary principle ensures stability from reign to reign, as reflected by the traditional cry: 'The King is dead; long live the King'. Unlike the victor at the next election, the identity of the next monarch (subject, of course, to the vagaries of life and death) is a forgone conclusion. Except in times of emergency or revolution, the next monarch is the oldest male heir, or the oldest child, of the existing monarch. The nation has plenty of time to get to know a future king. In turn, the monarch-to-be has time to prepare for the frustrations of a public life without political power.

A 'normal' politician?

If one of the key roles of any head of state is to symbolise the nation, a hereditary monarch may be more likely to approach psychological 'normalcy' than any elected politician. It takes a special type of person to aspire to national leadership. Combined with great qualities of power, confidence and idealism are often arrogance, obsession and destructive passion. To get to the top, it is often said, it helps to be a bastard. Even the most revered political leaders (such as Curtin, Chifley, Menzies, Churchill or De Gaulle) showed one-in-a-million qualities of drive, ambition, and self-belief. By contrast, the only qualification the monarch needs is to be of sound mind. It may be hard for the person-in-the-street to relate to the royal lifestyle but it is easy enough to relate to the royal personalities.

Years ago, commentators described the Queen's 'manifest sense of vocation, her perfect dignity... her obvious decency and, above all, her extraordinary stability of character' [Atkinson, p. 96]. Today, she is a dutiful, at times rather severe grandmother, seemingly a little perplexed at the way the world is changing – and under similar circumstances, who would not worry about the family 'firm'? Prince Charles is almost the archetype of modern man, unconvinced by tradition yet painfully idealistic and anxiously trying to please himself and everyone else at the same time. Charles seems almost the polar opposite of his father, Prince Philip, whose response to Gareth Evans' attempts to make small talk on the subject of Evans' frequent trips to the

UK to prepare the Australia Act was: 'big deal' [*Australian,* 13 September, 1997].

The unprecedented display of mourning for Princess Diana surprised the cynics and showed that, even as soap opera, royalty creates a powerful drama. In her journey from fairytale princess to scorned wife, single mum, and queen of hearts, Diana came to embody the angsts of the age. Her life comprised ordinary (rather than extraordinary) vices and virtues on display before billions of people. Without the royal connection, she could easily have been an anonymous Sloane Ranger. With it, her attempts to reconcile the pursuit of happiness and the call of duty fascinated half the world.

A real life family saga

As David Barnett has pointed out, the British never took to the Dagwood and Blondie comic strip because the Royals filled the papers with a competing 'real life' saga of (dysfunctional) family life. The Royals, he said:

> ... are quintessentially us. Dressed up in ermine, decked out with baubles, bearing medieval titles, but fundamentally an ordinary family. This, of course, is their strength.

Australian Financial Review, **4 September, 1997**

In the end, of course, the personality of the monarch is beside the point. Great qualities are a bonus – not a pre-requisite for the job. The hereditary nature of the Crown is essential to its success because it is the only way to keep competition – and politics – out of the selection process.

In fact, the hereditary principle has much more every-day operation than is commonly supposed. Who denies that Jamie Packer should inherit his father's business, that Melanie Howard should inherit her parents' acumen, or that Lisa Currie should pass on her looks to the next generation?

131

On the Australian waterfront, jobs are handed from father to son. So why not save the one principle which can give a result without a fight for the one job which must be filled without controversy?

In the late 20th century, constitutional monarchy is a thriving and relevant system of government for virtually half the countries of the OECD – the rich, industrial nations to whom Australia is accustomed to compare itself. In addition to Australia, Canada, New Zealand and the United Kingdom, countries such as Holland, Belgium, Sweden, Spain, Japan, Thailand and Malaysia are constitutional monarchies.

In each one of them, the Crown is an important source of unity and stability. The 'nation' can be a diffuse, hard-to-pin-down concept. And politicians are invariably too controversial to command the loyalty of an entire people. As a personality who 'stands' for the nation, a monarch can provide a personalised focus for loyalty. In getting elected and running a government, politicians make enemies. The nature of a constitutional monarch – who reigns but does not rule – ensures that society has at least one leader who is beyond political reproach.

In Australia, the Crown has a uniquely democratic flavour. Having distinguished Australian citizens represent the Queen (as governors or governors-general) makes identification with local concerns easier while still preserving the detachment from partisan politics which is always expected of the Crown.

The present system of Australian constitutional monarchy gives us something close to the best of all possible worlds. A hereditary monarch at the apex of our constitution gives us stability plus the absence of partisan politics from the nation's top job. A non-hereditary governor-general exercising all the Crown's powers under our constitution means that we are not dependent upon a dynastic lucky-dip and are largely insulated from the quirks of natural selection.

Regardless of the monarch's personal qualities, the Governor-General is always a distinguished Australian chosen by an Australian. It need not really matter to Australians if the monarch ever leaves something to be desired because all his or her duties are performed by the Australian Governor-General. When, on the other hand, the monarch is an outstanding individual, Australia is doubly fortunate.

Representing someone else tempers the vice-regal ego. Representing the Queen of Australia – who is universally acclaimed as a dutiful and faithful monarch – gives the Governor-General dignity. A head of state representing no-one but himself, surrounded by crowds and advisers, might get too big for his boots. A head of state representing a political party will face incessant demands to play favourites. Representing the Queen confers enough honour for the biggest ego – so that no governor-general has felt the need to compete with a prime minister. The job is big enough to appeal to almost every high achiever. Yet its derivative status means that no governor-general has mistaken himself for God.

CHAPTER TEN

The crystal ball

THE coming constitutional vote may very well be dominated by argument about foreigners. But instead of the 'foreign head of state' on which republicans wish to focus, debate is just as likely to compare Australia as it is with the various foreign republics we are sometimes asked to model ourselves upon.

Unfortunately for republicans, the most relevant international comparisons point to the daunting nature of their task. Canada is the society most like Australia to engage in a lengthy period of constitutional cogitation. Like Australia, the Canadians set out to establish 'complete independence' although, unlike Australia, they thought that this was established by 'bringing the Constitution home' (much as we did with the Australia Act) rather than by removing the 'foreign' Queen.

It is hard to say whether Canadians' desire to repatriate the Constitution was prompted by separatist stirrings in Quebec or helped to inflame them. In any event, after almost a generation of obsessively debating constitutional issues, Canada's continued existence as a nation is now in question. 'The Balkans without guns' (as expatriate Canadian academic Ian Holloway has described his own country) is a sobering lesson in the dangers of constitutional experiment and a reminder of the inherent dangers in stirring communities against each other.

Of the countries which have removed the Crown since the Second World War, only Ireland has been a functioning democracy throughout the period. Republican Pakistan has discriminated against non-Muslims and suffered various military coups. In South Africa, becoming a republic was an integral part of the apartheid program because the presence of the Crown made it more difficult to entrench and administer racist laws. Republican India was the shining third world democracy – until Prime Minister Gandhi prevailed upon a president elected by MPs to suspend the Constitution and declare a state of emergency. And in Fiji, in order to establish his race-based Constitution, General Rabuka found it necessary to remove the Crown altogether. In each case, the removal of the Crown has made it easier for politicians to exercise draconian powers. The monarch's continued existence at the apex of a system of Government means there are some things that politicians just cannot readily do.

A huge leap in the dark

It is one thing to dislike the antics of the junior Royals, grizzle about being in the slow lane at the Heathrow Airport customs queue, feel uncomfortable with toasting the Queen, and find the 'split personality' of the modern Crown (with the Governor-General exercising all the Queen's powers) hard to understand or explain. There would be few Australians to whom these sentiments are unknown. But changing the juridical basis of the Australian Constitution is a huge leap into the dark which, if mishandled, could threaten the stability of our system of government.

Although the coming vote for delegates to the Convention is far from the end of the constitutional debate – it is the beginning of the constitutional end-game. Although the Government's only current commitment is to hold the Convention, the Prime Minister has previously said that a failure to reach consensus at the Convention would be followed by an indicative plebiscite on various constitutional alternatives. If one option commanded broad support, a referendum on a specific republican model would follow.

This progression from debate over the issue, to decision in principle, to decision in detail is the logical way to settle the matter. One feature of this three stage process is that the republicans' task becomes more difficult at each step. The first step – the Convention vote – means persuading voters to support republican candidates (which should not be too hard, given the attitude of the media and republicans' ability to attract celebrity support). The second step – a plebiscite – means agreeing on a specific republican model (such as a president chosen by politicians rather than voters). The third step – a referendum – means convincing (at the very least) a majority of voters in a majority of States to support the dotted i's and crossed t's of a new constitution including questions about the extent of presidential power.

Unlike opinion polls which merely gauge support for the principle of a republic, or a plebiscite which would have political but not constitutional authority, a referendum would require voter endorsement of the specific republican option on offer. Changing the Constitution is not as simple as arranging a series of opinion polls nor choosing a can from the shelves of the constitutional supermarket. It cannot be done via a 'tick-a-box' option. The decision will finally be made when voters face a take-it-or-leave-it choice between what we have and a specific republican option worked out down to the last crucial comma.

Unless the supporters of the existing Australian Constitution can be persuaded that further resistance is futile, any referendum to become a republic will not simply pit republicans against monarchists. Most likely, monarchists and dissident republicans will line up against establishment republicans to argue against a republic with a president chosen by the politicians.

It is easy for individual Australians to conclude – because they thought Princess Di got a raw deal, hated Fleet Street's 'Aussie yobbo' type-casting or had any number of more substantial reasons – that Australia should become a republic. In a democracy, majorities must (and should) eventually get what they want. But the leaders of any society are required to put things into proper perspective. Given the difficulty of keeping politics out of any presidency and the problems transferring an appointed governor-general's powers to an elected president, the question to be posed is whether becoming a republic is more trouble than it's worth.

More trouble than it's worth?

There is an argument that becoming a republic is legally impossible. The the former Melbourne University constitutional expert, Professor Greg Craven said (echoing the warnings of Quick and Garran)

> It is a far from implausible suggestion, that a power of alteration, as a simple matter of semantics, does not include a power of fundamental transformation. For example, one may be said to be 'altering' a dress if one lets down the hem, but would it be mere alteration to turn a dress into a shirt?

Policy, Spring 1992

Craven suggests that the 'whiff of constitutional criminality may well go a long way to ensuring (a republic's political) downfall' – even if, in law, the High Court is unlikely to accept that the Crown is a 'fundamental term' of the Constitution.

McGarvie has said that:

Voters would be most reluctant to put in place a head of state whose position credible lawyers claimed would lack the legitimacy and authority of constitutional validity. They would fear what would happen to the whole system. The resolution of the republic issue would be distorted away from objective decision because many voters favouring a republic if other things were equal would vote against it.

Speech, 31 July, 1997

As Craven says, the High Court would be unlikely to find, as a matter of constitutional law, that Australia cannot become a republic. However, the mechanism under which a republic can validly be established is a more serious and pressing legal question. Becoming a republic means removing the Crown from the Constitution – including, if the job is to be done properly, changing the preamble which provides for 'one indissoluble Federal Commonwealth under the Crown...'.

Changing the preamble to the Australian Constitution would once have been a job for the Westminster Parliament. After the passage of the Australia Act, what was formerly the preserve of Westminster now vests in the processes of the Act. Section 15 (1) of the Australia Act specifies that any change to the Act requires the consent of all the States. In other words, while changing the Constitution itself only requires the consent of a majority of the people in a majority of the States (under section 128), changing the preamble to the Constitution may require the consent of all the States .

The Republic Advisory Committee sought the advice of the Acting Solicitor-General who said that section 15 (3) of the Australia Act allowed the Parliament, if given power under a section 128 referendum, to do anything that could be done under section 15 (1). He cited in support of this contention explanatory material provided during to Parliament on the Australia Acts Bills to the effect that section 15 (3):

> Leaves open the possibility that a future amendment to the Common-wealth Constitution using the section 128 referendum procedure might give the Commonwealth Parliament power to effect some alteration to the Australia Acts or the Statute of Westminster.
>
> Appendices, p. 302

Hence, the report concluded that the monarchy could be eliminated from the entire Australian polity by the ordinary federal referendum procedure of parliamentary legislation followed by referendum carried by a majority of the people in a majority of the States. This, the committee argued, was the effect at law. However, the committee conceded that any attempt to remove the Crown from the Constitutions of unwilling States could call into question the very basis of the federal compact. This argument 'may have some force' as a 'political proposition', the committee said [Report, p. 130].

The committee conceded that achieving a republic under section 15 (3) of the Australia Act without securing the consent of all the States was 'complicated' and 'might be seen as over-riding the interests of the States' [Report, p. 121]. To prevent this, the committee suggested that monarchist States might be allowed to exist within a republican Federation – although the resulting 'repubarchy' or 'monarlic' would be, the report conceded, a 'constitutional monstrosity'. In other words, becoming a republic, in political if not in legal fact, does seem to require the agreement of all the States and, therefore, has a 'degree of difficulty' exceeding that for constitutional change in general.

A constitutional monstrosity

The biggest obstacle to change is not legal but political: the electorate's well-established reluctance to tamper with the Constitution. The Australian record suggests that voters place the onus of proof and the burden of justification on the advocates of change. The Constitution does not have to be self-justifying – its critics have to justify themselves. This is the unavoidable dynamic of the referendum process and helps to explain why only eight of 42 referendum proposals have succeeded since 1901 and how the 1988 referendum proposals slipped from 80% support to 60% opposition in just a few months.

In politics, defence is much easier than attack. For the purposes of beating a referendum, opponents of a republic do not require a coherent critique – just a series of criticisms. To beat a referendum, the task of the anti-republicans is merely to highlight every potential problem, confident that there will be an objection that disturbs just about everyone. This does not make the republicans' job politically impossible – but it compounds the legal complications and makes any constitutional change more difficult than anything tried previously. This is as it should be, given what is at stake.

Even if Australians could more-or-less agree on the principle of becoming a republic, disagreement on the detail could indefinitely forestall its establishment. Almost as soon as the separate colonies were established, Australians agreed in principle that there should be some form of national Government but even under those circumstances Federation was nearly 50 years coming. There was very little outright opposition to Federation. The principle was as universally accepted as a political objective can be. The objections were in the detail: the site of the national capital, the powers of the Senate and the States' ability to tax. These problems meant a second vote in NSW, when the first plebiscite failed to achieve the necessary majority and almost left Western Australia out of the original compact.

In the absence of big changes in Australia's political culture, fair-minded republicans need to consider at which point campaigning for a republic becomes an exercise in destructive self-indulgence. If becoming a republic would solve urgent practical problems; if it were the unavoidable prerequisite of some urgent national task such as joining an Asian version of the European Union; if we had experienced a national catharsis such as a new Gallipoli, Australians might conclude that change was worth the trouble and expense. But Australia's current constitutional status has not stopped one migrant from coming, one business deal from proceeding, nor created even a metaphorical martyr to a republic.

Successful social reformers know how far to push their case. There has to be a point when republicans give up their crusade and focus on what they can achieve rather than what, in their version of a perfect world, they might still like to attain.

The eight successful proposals for constitutional change have mostly been constitutional house-keeping supported by both big parties. The support of those parties was not enough to save a 1967 proposal to synchronise Senate and House of Representatives elections – even though it was opposed only by the Democratic Labor Party and was put concurrently with the overwhelmingly successful proposal to count Aborigines as part of the Australian people. The Opposition managed to defeat the 1988 proposals (to guarantee freedom of religion, recognise local government and provide four year terms for Federal Parliament) by using their 'motherhood' nature against them – notwithstanding the fact that a four year term was actually part of Coalition policy!

State Constitutions have proved easier to change. In some cases, change can be effected by legislation only. In others, constitutional change requires only a majority at a state-wide vote (in contrast with the federal requirement of a majority of the people in a majority of the States). The most recent change to a State constitution was pitched as a limitation on the power of government. At the 1995 NSW State election, two concurrent referendum proposals received overwhelming support: one was to specify four year fixed terms for Parliament (thus removing the Premier's power to seek an election whenever most politically convenient); the other was to guarantee the independence of the judiciary (by preventing the Government from dismissing inconvenient judges by abolishing their jurisdictions).

At first glance, the success of New Zealand's proportional representation referendum proposal – which was opposed by both major parties – suggests that willingness to embrace radical change might be just over the political horizon. In New Zealand (as in Australia), a decade of 'reform' had given both political establishments a bad name. But many New Zealanders saw change as a way of giving all politicians the two fingered salute whereas support for a republic could seem less like rejecting a political system which has betrayed the public and more like the ultimate victory of a politically correct establishment way out of touch with the electorate.

The Report of the Republic Advisory Committee helped to illustrate the difficulty of the republicans' task: first, by its length – a 32 page Constitution required a 203 page report plus a 341 page appendix to outline options for minimal change; and second, by its reluctance to make firm recommendations. The report's length testifies to the thoroughness of its authors as well as to the complexity of their task. But the imagery of Lloyd Waddy holding a pocket-sized copy of the Constitution in one hand while trying to lift the three volume report in the other, helped to demonstrate his point that change was no easy matter.

Although winning delegates to the Convention is the easiest part of the republicans' electoral task (the political equivalent, if you like, of the trek from Kathmandu to the Everest base camp), the end game will cast its shadow even over the beginning of the process. Current opinion polls suggest that republicans should win a majority of delegates to the Constitutional Convention. But beyond the proposition that if Australia were to start again from Year Zero, it would be unlikely to choose a monarchical system of government, any sort of consensus on becoming a republic will be very hard to achieve.

The republican movement estimates that slightly over half the appointed delegates to the Constitutional Convention lean towards a republic [*Bulletin,* 9 September, 1997]. But even if republican candidates win 60% of the elected positions, there will be nothing like a consensus in support of a republic (especially if the voluntary postal ballot attracts a poor turn-out).

Paul Kelly says that, post-Convention, the Prime Minister has the option of: moving to a multiple choice plebiscite (which will probably confirm popular support for an elected presidency); offering voters an 'either/or' choice between the existing system and a president picked by the politicians (which maximises the chances of the monarchy); or putting what he thinks will be the Convention preference for the 'Keating model' straight to a referendum [*Australian,* 17 September, 1997]. Michelle Grattan says that Howard 'needs a credible, well thought out Convention position', but admits that the debate becomes 'highly complicated once past the baseline 'Australian head of state' question' [*Australian Financial Review*, 15 September, 1997].

The Press Gallery line is that the Prime Minister must sooner or later face up to the inevitability of a republic. But 'status quo or republic' is not the only choice on offer. There are other options which could be presented to the Convention and which would avoid the hard choice between a system which some say gives too much authority to the Queen and a system which others say gives too much power to a president.

CHAPTER ELEVEN

An Australian head of state

A S a kind of legal fiction that enables us to have a constitutional head of state, appointed in much the same way as a judge, and subsequently outside the political process, the monarchy continues to serve an important role – even if (as Hirst argues) it has become a contentious rather than a unifying symbol in our civic life. Even if over 50% of Australians continued to tell pollsters that they would prefer to change the existing constitutional arrangements, the system could endure. After all, Australia has flourished well enough under the 'foreign queen' and even the republican movement says that only the symbols of our system of government need to be changed.

A system which has put Sir Zelman Cowen, Sir Ninian Stephen, Bill Hayden and Sir William Deane into Yarralumla cannot be accused of failure to produce first class citizens in our top job. Some governors-general will be more outspoken, or better regarded, or more taken to the hearts of the Australian people than others. In law, they will represent a monarch who mostly resides in a country with which Australia has close cultural ties but no formal constitutional links. In fact, notwithstanding republican grumbling, they will represent the Australian people in ways which would be impossible for elected politicians.

Our existing system of government – which almost no-one admits wanting to change – could continue indefinitely. Australians could continue to live with a widening gap between the formal authority of the Crown and the Queen's real power. The critics could continue to tolerate our existing constitutional arrangements, as they always have in the past.

Alternatively, we could try to solve the problem of a diminishing crown by abolishing it all together (as republicans argue). Or we could try to refurbish the Crown as an Australian institution. As an alternative to becoming a republic, the Convention should consider the case for bringing constitutional theory and practice into closer harmony without abandoning existing symbols or our traditional system of government.

Most prominent republicans say that they support our system of government – but object to a 'foreign queen'. Most prominent anti-republicans say that their loyalty is to a constitution which provides 'leadership beyond politics' – rather than to the House of Windsor. If the chief arguments on both sides are to be taken at face value, there are ways around the issue which involve modifying the existing system without actually becoming a republic. This is what former Liberal Party Director Andrew Robb seemed to be seeking when he recently declared that 'it is time that we had our very own Australian head of state who reigns but does not rule' but that he would not join the Australian Republican Movement [*Australian*, 12 September, 1997].

An Australian king?

'If there was an Australian monarchy' said Nick Greiner once, 'I'd be happy as Larry' [*Sydney Morning Herald*, 19 June, 1993]. Alan Atkinson has suggested that the Queen could be asked to agree to changing the order of succession so that the monarchy in Australia passes to another branch of the Royal Family.

A new and separate monarchy could be reshaped to Australian specifications so as to make it much simpler and cheaper than the British model.

Atkinson, pp 128-9

Even if there were a sentimental case for persuading a member of the House of Windsor to renounce his or her claim to the British throne in return for becoming King or Queen of Australia (so that our traditional links could be honoured at the same time as they were cut) such an implausible 'solution' is unlikely to be accepted. Some republicans chafe under the checks and balances on executive government built into our existing system and would reject an alternative which granted their professed but not their real goals. Most republicans are profoundly uncomfortable with the hereditary principle (and even some monarchists are pleased that it operates at Buckingham Palace rather than Yarralumla). Perhaps the biggest difficulty would be deciding whom to choose. Suggestions for replacing the House of Windsor with an Australian monarch would probably range from Cathy Freeman to Bob and Blanche before dissolving into jokes.

If an Australian monarch is unlikely, there are ways to give the monarch of Australia more of an Australian accent. Australia could make more of the House of Windsor. If the monarchy is mostly seen through the prism of the tabloid press, that is partly because, in Australia at least, there are very few competing images. In Britain, the Queen has a hectic round of community engagements. In Australia, members of the Royal Family often seem like up-market tourists even when they are here for hospital visits and CWA meetings.

Seeing more of the Queen?
In the 1960s, as the British Empire dissolved, the old Common-wealth bonds loosened, and the monarchy was recognised

THESE ARE THE
PEOPLE ALL
FORLORN...

WHO BUY THE
MAGS.....

..THAT PURCHASE
THE PICS...

FROM PAPARAZZI.

CREATED BY
THE PEOPLE...

WHO HOUND CELEBRITY...

ALL FORLORN...

WHO BUY
THE MAGS.....

(juridically at least) as an international rather than a British institution, there was at least one proposal that the Queen should spend more time outside Britain [see Atkinson, p. 84]. Subsequently, there has been talk of the Royal Family purchasing a residence in Australia which the Queen or Prince Charles would occupy for some time every year.

It makes sense, the argument runs, for the Queen of Australia to reside here for at least a few weeks every year. The Queen currently moves between Buckingham Palace and her residences at Windsor, Balmoral and Sandringham, depending on the time of year and the exigencies of State, so – at the risk of over-crowding an already packed schedule – why not add an Australian home to the Royal Progress?

An alternative to making more of the monarch is making more of the Governor-General. Because the Governor-General is hand-picked, so to speak, to be an adornment to our society – and is not the product of number-crunching or factional wheeler-dealing – there is a strong likelihood that he or she will be the very best type of Australian. Comparing governors-general with prime ministers over the past two decades, it is a fair bet that most Australians would be happy to have seen and heard more of our heads of state and (perhaps) less of our heads of government. Similarly, comparing governors-general with individual members of the extended royal clan, many Australians would be glad that we had a distinguished citizen of our own in residence at Yarralumla.

Ever since Australians have regularly filled the post, the Governor-General has been a citizen of distinction. On great national occasions, when the Australian people assemble for celebration or commemoration, the Governor-General – rather than the Prime Minister – could take the most prominent role. The Governor-General, for instance, should open the 2000 Olympics. If he can sign Australian bills into law, he can certainly say the few words necessary to launch the Olympics. The Queen (or perhaps Prince William) would be a welcome guest of honour at other Olympic events but the Governor-General should officiate at the opening to ensure that no-one confuses Australia's constitutional arrangements with Britain's.

Making more of the Governor-General

There is an argument that, whatever more far-reaching changes might one day be made to the Constitution, Australians should promptly ensure that our constitutional forms better reflect our constitutional substance. Let's remove any doubt and declare that the Governor-General is Australia's head of state in law as well as fact. Such a proposal, in fact, is probably necessary if the Constitutional Convention is not to bog down in the constitutional equivalent of trench warfare.

The dynamic of a Constitutional Convention with large numbers of genuinely uncommitted delegates is more likely to result in a compromise than a win for either side. Even if the pro and anti-republican forces could maintain strict discipline among their own delegates, the presence of appointed delegates of great personal authority means that the Convention will be quite different from a parliament where MPs can be relied upon to toe a party line.

It is a fair bet, given the different strands of thought in both the republican and anti-republican camps – that the mood of the Convention will be to keep the existing Constitution as far as possible while simultaneously providing for an Australian head of state. Because a series of set piece arguments followed by bitter personal exchanges and hotly contested ballots is unlikely to advance the cause of national unity, it is reasonable to expect that delegates will be interested in alternatives to 'either/or' and 'all-or-nothing' outcomes.

The Convention should be seeking to resolve the alleged problem of 'outside interference' from a 'foreign head of state' while answering the monarchist challenge to preserve intact the strengths of our existing system. It should consider the merits of a new Head of State Bill (attached as Appendix Two to this book) providing that the head of state, under the Australian Constitution, is the Governor-General. If this were regarded as insufficiently authoritative, the Head of State Act could be entrenched in the Constitution through a referendum (as provided in Appendix Three).

A Head of State Bill, if passed into law by the Parliament or entrenched in the Constitution by the people, would make no difference whatsoever to our existing system of government. To the extent that this is not already the case, it would grant the republicans' desire for an Australian head of state.

The draft bill goes further and provides that the Governor-General may also be known as 'President of Australia'. Any such president would exercise the same powers as the

Governor-General because the title is all that has been added. The Governor-General would remain 'Governor-General and Commander-in-Chief' but would, in addition, also become 'President and head of state'.

Nothing could be more natural, in an ultra minimal monarchy, to refer to the representative of the Crown as a president – especially given the common usage of the term 'president' within our existing system of government (as in President of the Senate, President of the Court of Appeal and so on). To those who ask: where does this leave the Queen? – it leaves her exactly where she is, Queen of Australia no more and no less.

This change eliminates any doubt or ambiguity about a 'foreign' head of state. Henceforth, the Australian head of state, under Australian law, will be the Australian Governor-General/President. It is not a republic because it does not remove the Crown. Unlike the McGarvie option canvassed earlier, it does not remove the Queen either. But it provides the republicans with what they say they want, 'a resident for president'.

A resident for president

When Federal Schools Minister David Kemp followed by Deputy Prime Minister Tim Fischer first hinted at a solution along these lines, they were welcomed as converts to republicanism. In fact, this is an ultra-minimal monarchy rather than a republic because the Crown would remain in the Constitution and the Queen would continue to appoint the head of state on prime ministerial advice (even though the Governor-General is potentially re-badged as President of Australia).

It should be stressed that such a change is not required by any defect in Australia's governance. The Governor-General is already Australia's head of state in every meaningful sense. As mainstream republicans concede, there is nothing wrong with the Australian system of government that becoming a republic is guaranteed to fix. The only pressing problem with the Australian Constitution is that about half the Australian people have been persuaded that they should no longer be happy with it – and this change is designed to fix that without altering anything else.

The challenge is to solve the problem of the 'foreign queen' in ways which do not alienate the millions of Australian who (perhaps with even stronger passion) cleave to the Constitution we have. Formalising the Governor-General's position as head of state could be the public acknowledgment of existing constitutional reality needed to resolve the debate, give all participants a win, and allow Australia's leaders to move on to more pressing problems.

In the sense that it would bring constitutional theory more perfectly in line with constitutional practice (and meet the mood for a significant public declaration), any such move would resemble the Australian ratification of the Statute of Westminster ten years after its passage through the British Parliament. In the sense that it would not add to (nor detract from) our existing constitutional amenity but would resolve a nagging emotional or psychic issue, it would be the constitutional equivalent of slashing the Gordian knot.

Why do we have to resolve the constitutional issue? Because it's there. The ultra-minimal monarchy provides a way to climb the constitutional Everest without ever leaving home. Australia can have an Australian head of state while keeping every dotted 'i' and crossed 't' of its current Constitution in what amounts to the best of all constitutional worlds.

The Head of State Bill achieves the objectives of the republican movement without the need to embark on an uncertain and potentially hazardous re-definition of the Governor-General's existing powers and without the need to become more of a republic than we actually are. By establishing a head of state who is 'one of us' without altering any of the substantive provisions of the Constitution, it also avoids offending the supporters of the constitutional status quo.

The problem with becoming a republic in the foreseeable future is that millions of Australians will feel betrayed. The problem with remaining precisely as we are is that millions of Australians no longer support what should be country's foundation document. A liberal democracy cannot leave even substantial minorities permanently alienated – hence the need to win the constitutional war, but not in a way which replaces one disaffected group with another.

It would be surprising if any proposition to emerge from the Convention (and subsequently accepted by the Australian Parliament or people) marked the end of Australia's constitutional journey. This proposal may not solve all problems for all time but it can solve one problem for our time and that is all this generation can reasonably hope to achieve.

REFERENCES

Alan Atkinson, *The Muddle Headed Republic*, OUP, 1993

Geoffrey Blainey, *A Shorter History of Australia*, William Heinemann, 1994

Evans et al, *Australia's Constitution – Time for a Change?*, Allen and Unwin, 1983

Gareth Grainger and Kerry Jones (Eds), *The Australian Constitutional Monarchy*, ACM Publishing, 1994

John Hirst, *A Republican Manifesto*, OUP, 1994

Donald Horne and others, *The Coming Republic*, Sun Australia, 1992

Paul Keating, *The Way Forward*, Statement to Parliament, 7 June, 1995

Paul Keating, *The Way Forward* (Questions and Answers), Statement tabled in Parliament, 7 June, 1995

John Kerr, *Matters for Judgment*, Macmillan, 1978

Richard McGarvie, *The McGarvie Proposal for a Republican Equivalent of our Present System of Democracy* (various papers collated by their author), 1997

Geoffrey Partington, *The Australian Nation – Its British and Irish Roots*, Australian Scholarly Publishing, 1994

Malcolm Turnbull, *The Reluctant Republic*, Mandarin, 1994

Turnbull et al, *An Australian Republic – The Report*, Commonwealth of Australia, 1993

Turnbull et al, *An Australian Republic – The Appendices*, Commonwealth of Australia, 1993

Gough Whitlam, *The Truth of the Matter*, Penguin, 1983

George Winterton, *We, the People*, Allen and Unwin, 1994

Constitution Alteration (Australian Crown and Australian head of state) 1997

No.   , 1997

A Proposed Law to alter the Constitution to provide for an Australian Crown and an Australian head of state and for related matters

Contents

A Proposed Law to alter the Constitution to provide for an Australian Crown and an Australian head of state and for related matters

WHEREAS Australia has enjoyed nearly a century of stable government under the Crown and evolved peacefully from a self-governing dominion within the British Empire to a fully independent member of the Commonwealth of Nations;

AND WHEREAS the Australian nation is drawn from the peoples of the entire world who have built on a British heritage and the generosity of the Aboriginal people to create a society which is both free and fair;

AND WHEREAS the centenary of federation is a suitable time to acknowledge the complete independence of the Australian Crown and the autonomy of the Governor-General who exercises all the powers of the Crown under the Constitution.

The Parliament of Australia, with the approval of the electors, as required by the Constitution, therefore enacts:

1 **Short title**
This act may be cited as the Constitution Alteration (Australian Crown and Australian head of state) 1997.

2 **Legislative power**
Section 1 of the Constitution is altered by omitting 'Queen' and substituting 'Governor-General'.

3 **Governor-General and Constitutional Council**
The Constitution is altered by omitting section 2 and substituting the following section:
Governor-General and Constitutional Council
'2. (1) There shall be a Governor-General who shall represent the Crown in the Commonwealth and who shall be, in recognition of the powers and functions granted to the Governor-General by this Constitution, the head of state of the Commonwealth.

(2) The Governor-General shall be appointed and, if necessary, dismissed, by a Constitutional Council acting on the advice of the Prime Minister.

(3) The Constitutional Council shall consist of the three Australian citizens who have most recently retired as Governor of a State.

(4) The Governor-General shall be an Australian citizen.

(5) The Constitutional Council may appoint such other persons, on the advice of the Prime Minister, to administer the Government of the Commonwealth in the absence from Australia, or the death or incapacity, of the Governor-General.'

4 Salary of Governor-General
Section 3 of the Constitution is altered by omitting 'to the Queen'.

5 Provisions relating to Governor-General
Section 4 of the Constitution is altered by omitting 'Queen' and substituting 'Constitutional Council'.

6 Qualifications of members
Section 34 of the Constitution is altered by omitting 'a subject of the Queen' and substituting 'an Australian citizen'.

7 Disqualification
Section 44 of the Constitution is altered by omitting 'Queen's' (wherever occurring).

8 Disagreement between the Houses
Section 57 of the Constitution is altered by omitting 'for the Queen's assent' and substituting 'for assent'.

9 Assent to bills
The Constitution is altered by omitting the following words from the first paragraph of section 58: 'for the Queen's assent', 'in the Queen's name' and, 'or that he reserves the law for the Queen's pleasure.'.

10 Disallowance by the Queen
The Constitution is altered by omitting section 59.

11 Signification of Queen's pleasure on Bills reserved
The Constitution is altered by omitting section 60.

12 Executive power
Section 61 of the Constitution is altered by omitting 'Queen' and 'Queen's' and substituting 'Crown' and 'Crown's' respectively.

13 Ministers of State
Section 64 of the Constitution is altered by omitting 'Queen's'.

14 Salaries of Ministers
Section 66 of the Constitution is altered by omitting 'to the Queen,'.

15 Command of naval and military forces
Section 68 of the Constitution is altered by omitting 'as the Queen's representative'.

16 Appellate jurisdiction of High Court
Section 73 of the Constitution is altered by omitting the second and third paragraphs of the section.

17 Appeal to Queen in Council
The Constitution is altered by omitting section 74.

18 Rights of residents in States
Section 117 of the Constitution is altered by omitting 'Queen' (wherever occurring) and substituting 'Crown'.

19 Government of territories
Section 122 of the Constitution is altered by omitting 'by the Queen'.

20 Authority to Governor-General to appoint deputies
The Constitution is altered by omitting section 126 and substituting the following section:

'126. The Governor-General may appoint any person, or any persons jointly or severally, to be his or her deputy or deputies within any part of the Commonwealth, and in that capacity to exercise during the pleasure of the Governor-General such powers and functions of the Governor-General as he thinks fit to assign to such deputy or deputies; but the appointment of such deputy or deputies shall not affect the exercise by the Governor-General himself or herself of any power or function.'

21 Mode of altering the Constitution
Section 128 of the Constitution is altered by omitting 'for the Queen's'.

22 Alteration of Schedule to the Constitution
The Constitution is altered by omitting the Schedule and the Note to the Schedule and substitution the following Schedule:

'SCHEDULE

OATH

I, A.B., do sear that I will faithfully uphold the Constitution of the Commonwealth of Australia according to law. SO HELP ME GOD!

AFFIRMATION

I, A.B., do solemnly and sincerely affirm and declare that I will faithfully uphold the Constitution of the Commonwealth of Australia according to law.'.

The Australian head of state Bill 1997

No. , 1997

A Bill for an Act for an Australian head of state

Contents

A Bill for an Act for and Australian head of state

WHEREAS it is provided by section 2 of the Constitution that a Governor-General appointed by the Queen is to be Her Majesty's representative in the Commonwealth;

AND WHEREAS the Constitution is otherwise silent upon the designation and identity of the head of state of Australia;

AND WHEREAS it is desirable to clarify the said designation and identity of Australia's head of state;

AND WHEREAS by virtue of the powers and functions conferred upon and exercisable by the Governor-General by and under the Constitution, the Governor-General is alone able to act as the head of state of Australia;

AND WHEREAS for more abundant clarity of the position and powers and functions of the Governor-General under the Constitution, it is now expedient to declare the identity of the head of state and to provide for certain additional titles to be bestowed upon the Governor-General.

The Parliament of Australia enacts:

1 Short title
This Act may be cited as *The Australian head of state Act 1997*.

2 Commencement
This Act commences on the day on which it receives the Royal Assent.

3 Declaration of Governor-General as head of state
In recognition of the powers and functions granted to the Governor-General by the Constitution, the Parliament declares that the Governor-General is the head of state of the Commonwealth.

4 Additional titles of the Governor-General
Whilst a Governor-General holds office as such under the Constitution:

(a) it shall be lawful on all occasions to refer to the Governor-General by the title and designation of 'Head of state of Australia';

(b) it shall be lawful on all occasions to refer to the Governor-General as 'President of the Commonwealth'; and

(c) it shall be lawful to refer to the Governor-General by one or more of his titles on any or all occasions.

5 Constitutional Validity

(1) Nothing in this Act shall be taken to alter, amend or affect the Constitution in any way.

(2) In particular nothing in this Act shall be taken to alter, amend, affect, derogate from or enhance any rights, powers, functions or duties of any person in relation to, or arising from, the Constitution.

Constitution Alteration (Australian head of state) 1997

No. , 1997

A Proposed Law to alter the Constitution to provide for an Australian head of state

Contents

A Proposed Law to alter the Constitution to provide for an Australian head of state

WHEREAS it is provided by section 2 of the Constitution that a Governor-General appointed by the Queen is to be Her Majesty's representative in the Commonwealth;

AND WHEREAS the Constitution is otherwise silent upon the designation and identity of the head of state of Australia;

AND WHEREAS it is desirable to clarify the said designation and identity of Australia's head of state;

AND WHEREAS by virtue of the powers and functions conferred upon and exercisable by Governor-General and under the Constitution, the Governor-General is alone able to act as the head of state of Australia;

AND WHEREAS for more abundant clarity of the position and powers and functions of the Governor-General under the Constitution, it is now expedient to declare the identity of the head of state and to provide for certain additional titles to be bestowed upon the Governor-General.

The Parliament of Australia, with the approval of the electors, as required by the Constitution, enacts:

1 Short title

This Act may be cited as the *Constitution Alteration (Australian head of state) 1997*.

2 Governor-General

The Constitution is altered by adding the following paragraph to section 2:

'The Governor-General shall preside over the affairs of the Commonwealth and at all times perform the duties of head of state in Australia and accordingly may at all times during his tenure be referred to as Head of state of Australia or President of the Commonwealth in addition to, or instead of, his other styles or titles.'.